Powerful Thinking on Purpose

How to BE More Positive and GET More of What You Want

by
Wendy Merron

ISBN: 0615613454

ISBN: 13: 9780615613451

To my father, Julio

Table of Contents

Introduction

Jennifer was concerned about her job and her finances. Each day when she listened to the news, she felt more and more stressed. She couldn't stop worrying about the economy, global warming, and terrorism.

By the time she came to me, she was so anxious that she was even hesitant to plan her family's summer vacation.

Her thoughts were uncharacteristically out of control and were affecting her sleep, her job, and her family. She felt stuck and couldn't stop worrying.

Through the process I explain in this book, Jennifer was able to regain control of her thoughts. She stayed focused on areas that she could influence. In addition to feeling less stressed, she began to sleep better, focus better at work, and feel more optimistic about her future. She felt calmer, happier, and more positive.

Jennifer is one of many clients who experienced a significant improvement throughout her life as a result of using Powerful Thinking on Purpose.

Have you ever met anyone who you consider to be a negative thinker? I'm sure you can think of a friend, relative, or co-worker who seems to always think this way—continually moping about something going wrong, how difficult things are, or complaining how others treat him. You probably don't enjoy spending lots of time with this person, but when you do, does the thought ever cross your mind, *"If he could just think more positively, things might be different"*?

Most likely, you aren't as negative as this person, but I'll bet you can recall times in your life when you were anxious and worried that things wouldn't work out the way you wanted. Regardless of what actually happened, you probably spent countless minutes, even hours, in the throes of bad feelings.

If I told you that changing your thoughts can not only make you feel better, but also change what happens in your life, would you believe me? I hope so, because it's true. Not because I say it's true. It's true because millions of people over the years have experienced major changes in their lives when they learned to change their thoughts. Many have written books to share these concepts with their fellow man, just as I'm sharing this with you now.

As a Coach and Board Certified Hypnotist, my primary goal is to empower my clients with ways to reduce stress and improve their lives. I do this by helping them discover that their thoughts and the things they imagine in their mind have a profound effect on their lives. I've helped thousands of people to feel better and achieve their goals.

I don't mean to sound like I'm an amazing person just because I've helped so many improve their lives. It's simply that the tools and techniques I teach clients are incredibly effective and easy to use.

Most people who seek me out are quite successful in more than one aspect of their life, whether personal or professional. The common thread is that all of them are frustrated and stuck in one area.

When clients learn and use the powerful technique outlined in this book, they quickly notice an improvement in their feelings – they are aware that they are now reacting differently. Their old stressors no longer rule their lives because they have intentionally changed their thoughts.

Most mention at their second session that while their life situation continues to remain the same, they notice that they are reacting differently. One client said it was as if a switch turned on that cleared her mind of her grey clouds. She remarked that she felt much more positive and open to possibilities that things would be OK.

Throughout this book, not only will you learn why it's important to change your thinking, you'll learn how to integrate a simple and powerful tool into your life to help you change your thoughts.

This book teaches you to transition from the way you currently think to intentionally transforming your life through Powerful Thinking on Purpose. When you hold positive thoughts in your mind and focus on what you want, you will achieve your goals without struggling. The trick is to purposefully change your thoughts by replacing them with powerful thoughts.

My goal is to help you feel happier and to utilize these proven helpful techniques to improve your life. As you read, I expect you will have a few "AHA" moments, where the knowledge that you already have becomes amazingly clear. You may also have a few affirming moments when you realize that you are on the path of becoming a positive thinker.

It's difficult to explain what positive thinking means. Most of us describe positive thinking as the *opposite* of negative thinking:

Positive thinking is when you don't think about negative thoughts.

Positive thinking is when you make sure you do not think about what you don't want.

The definition of the word "positive" according to the Merriam-Webster Dictionary is:

Positive: Contributing toward or characterized by increase or progression

To me, positive thinking means to concentrate on something that is constructive and good. It means that you are using your thoughts to move forward in the direction of your goals and desires.

Powerful Thinking is a technique that you will discover which helps you maintain a positive focus on a specific, desired outcome. Powerful Thinking on Purpose is an elegant technique that is easy to learn and implement. Once you begin to use it and notice how your life feels better, it will be easy for you to remember to use it daily.

By the end of this book, you will be creating new, powerful positive thoughts to replace old, useless, negative ones. When you start to practice, you may notice a feeling of lightness and happiness that you haven't felt for a long time. Feeling positive is one of the best feelings around. What's wonderful is that the more you practice, the more positive you'll find yourself.

Does this mean that when you think positively, you become unrealistic, and overly optimistic? Will you be viewing the world through "rose colored glasses"? Not necessarily. In order to be effective, your positive thoughts need to be believable.

In my definition, thinking powerfully is more of a process than an end result. If I told you that every thought that goes through my mind is positive, I'd be lying. If I told you that once you learn these techniques, you will never have to think about your thoughts again, it would be untrue.

The reality is that you have thousands of thoughts each day and you are always going to experience negative thoughts. It's totally normal. The difference is that you will now be more and more aware of your thoughts every day. This new awareness will allow you to make the powerful thought changes you need to feel good and create the life you desire.

It goes without saying that if you don't change what you are doing now, your life will continue to be the same.

The processes that you'll be learning are approaches that I have discovered or developed throughout the years during my ongoing personal search for more happiness. These are also the same tools and techniques that I teach each and every client in my practice. Some of the processes I describe you will use daily and some you won't. Take the ones you like the most and use them to propel your life toward feeling more optimistic and achieving your goals.

There are dozens of ways to change and choose your thoughts. This book is a compilation of the ways that I have found to be the easiest and most effective. To become a powerful thinker is to consciously control and direct your thoughts about the future to achieve your goals without struggling.

When you take your time to learn and use these techniques, your life will change. Among the many benefits of positive thinking are:

- Improved health
- More happiness
- Greater satisfaction
- Ability to see opportunities
- Getting what you want
- More enjoyment
- More fun

Powerful Thinking on Purpose is the bridge from your current reality to believable outcomes. Will you wake up tomorrow and be richer, healthier, thinner, or funnier? Probably not. But you can wake up tomorrow feeling better, more optimistic, and take action on the opportunities that will propel your future.

Chapter 1

Everything Starts With a Thought

A thought is what happens when your mind actively forms connected ideas. Merriam Webster defines thinking as "to form or have in the mind" and a thought as 1: the process of thinking, 2: serious consideration, 3: reasoning power, 4: the power to imagine.

Unfortunately we cannot see a thought, but we can see the results of a thought. Every new thought creates a new neural pathway in your mind. Neural pathways look a bit like tiny roots growing. Your mind is full of them. When you have the same thought over and over, the neural pathway becomes thicker. Using medical technology, we can actually view these neural pathways forming in the mind.

Thoughts don't have physical structure, weight, or color. Some thoughts are like wisps of smoke, disappearing before we notice them. Other thoughts feel so stuck in our minds that it seems it would be easier to move a sleeping elephant. Many thoughts repeat over and over in our minds. No one has been able to prove the existence of thoughts, but we do know they exist.

Every day we repeat hundreds of thoughts. How many times have you noticed repeating one thought to yourself?

DID YOU KNOW?

If you have a thought every 1 to 4 seconds, you have between 14,400 – 57,600 thoughts per day.

Most of these are repetitive negative thoughts.

Here are some repetitive negative thoughts about the future you might recognize:

> *I'll never get promoted.*
>
> *I can't do this.*
>
> *I'm worried I'll lose my job.*
>
> *I'm afraid I'll get sick.*
>
> *What if I can't reach my quota?*
>
> *I'm worried I'll never lose weight.*
>
> *No one will ever choose me.*
>
> *What if I can't do this?*

Here are some repetitive positive thoughts about the future:

Hey! How come there are no repetitive positive thoughts up above?

There are none because most people don't have positive thoughts about the future that they repeat throughout the day. Take a moment and think about your future. What was your first thought? Did you imagine a pleasant scene or one that made you worry?

Do you want to be just like the others who never get out of their negative thinking box? Of course you don't. You want your life to be satisfying, fulfilling, and full of love. Other people live the lives they desire, why can't you?

The people who are fulfilled and enjoying their lives are doing something differently than you. They are choosing to direct their thoughts every day.

These highly successful people are the ones who know how to create and repeat positive thoughts in their minds. They know the value of taking control of their thoughts rather than letting their thoughts control them. This is what Powerful Thinking on Purpose will teach you.

"You have the tools necessary to establish a solid foundation and move your life in an upward spiral of self-fulfillment. Once you begin, it becomes easier and easier to improve your life."

-DAVE BRAXTON, Business Owner-Investor-Advisor, Co-Founder of HighPerformanceU.com

Many athletes use the power of thought to help them during a game. Imagine that your favorite basketball player is sitting on a bench in the locker room right before an important game. He's hunched forward and his head is in his hands. He's worrying that he will throw the ball and it will miss. In his mind he throws the ball and watches it bounce off the rim of the basket. He can't stop this image from repeating in his mind. The more he thinks about it, the more worried he feels.

It's now time to play. He walks onto the court trying to shake this negative image out of his mind. What kind of game do you think he'll play? Most likely not his best.

Now imagine that the same basketball player is sitting on the bench prior to the game. This time his eyes are shut and he has a slight smile on his face. He is actively creating a short, powerful film in his mind. In his film he sees himself throwing the ball and feels his hands punching the air with excitement as the basketball cleanly swishes through the net. In the background he hears the crowd cheering and feels his teammates slap him on the shoulder. His face breaks into a wide grin as he imagines his success.

Ready to get out and play, he struts onto the court smiling, shoulders back, feeling confident. Do you think that he'll play a great game? Of course he will!

We can learn two important facts from our basketball player:

1. Whatever he creates in his mind is bound to happen.
2. He feels better when he chooses to focus on what he wants.

Some negative thoughts can seriously affect the physical body. The longer these negative thoughts and feelings stay stuck inside, the worse someone can feel. Years of guilt and regret can even manifest in physical ailments like stomach problems and chronic headaches.

Over time, repetitive worries and stress can even cause physical problems such as Irritable Bowel Syndrome or worse.

Another negative thought that can cause physical sensations is one of fear. A particularly common one is the fear of public speaking.

Have you ever known someone who was extremely nervous and anxious about giving an upcoming presentation or speech? Repetitive negative thoughts about an upcoming presentation can cause some people to feel so nervous and anxious that they can lose sleep and worse, won't even show up for their own presentation.

You Can Be in Control of Your Thoughts

This may sound silly, but being aware of your thoughts is not as easy as it seems. Frankly, it's easy to go through your day running from here to there and keeping your life together, all the while not being aware of one thought. You might notice that you are aware of how you feel—good, calm, anxious, frustrated, etc.—but not aware of your thoughts.

Once you are aware of your thoughts, it's easy to take the next step: changing them. Keep in mind that as you are becoming more aware, it's important to remember that you can be in *total control* of your thoughts.

Anytime you can take a deep breath and acknowledge something good and beneficial in your life, you are doing your mind and body a lovely favor. This is because you are taking a brief moment from your busy, stressful day to focus on a thought that feels good. Thoughts that feel good translate into a body that feels good. Your body is hardwired to work this way.

NOW YOU KNOW

One beneficial way to think is to be mindful of your thoughts. Taking a moment to be attentive and aware of positive things going around you is good practice and can even help reduce your stress levels.

Acknowledging thoughts such as *"I am enjoying this beautiful warm day"* or *"I feel grateful and happy"* can propel you forward too.

You Always Have a Choice

You can choose to think about the future in a negative way:

I'm really nervous about giving my presentation to the board next week.

You can choose to think about the future in a positive way:

I'm so glad I have an opportunity to speak to the board next week.

You can choose to think about the past and have a positive feeling:

I'm so glad I bought my new car.

You can choose to think about the past and experience a negative feeling:

I wish I had never wasted my time in that class.

Did you notice the most repeated word above? The word is *"choose."*

Of course, you can also choose to think about the present moment, which has tremendous benefits. This is called "mindful thinking." This way of thinking invites reflection in the moment and ultimately creates an implicit awareness of more than one perspective. There are hundreds of books, web sites, and many classes available to learn mindful thinking. For our purposes though, we will be focusing only on negative and positive thoughts.

Most people have no idea that they can control their thoughts. For many, it's a revelation when they learn that they can *stop a negative thought* and choose to replace it with a positive thought.

The reality is that our thoughts are the one thing that we have full control over. No one can ever take this away from you. By the conclusion of this book, you will choose to change your thoughts every day and you'll be surprised when you notice how easily and rapidly your outlook on life improves.

Let's review the different kinds of thoughts about the future:

1. Negative thoughts about the future.
2. Positive thoughts about the future.

Here is the problem with negative thoughts about the future:

**Every time one enters your mind,
it's guaranteed to make you feel bad.**

Throughout this book, you will be learning the easiest way to change your negative thoughts into positive thoughts. The beauty of Powerful Thinking on Purpose is that it is simple and it always works. *Whether you believe it works or not.*

Just as you have bought this book to explore new ways to improve your life, you can easily choose to change and improve your thoughts.

For example, if you are in sales, you might have been saying to yourself:

I'm worried that I won't make a sale today.

You'll be able to quickly change your thought to one that empowers you and causes a good feeling in the moment. For example, when you choose to think:

I'm looking forward to making a sale today.

you are creating the space to be the best you can be and close that sale. You'll feel great while you think about your positive outcome and all the good things that will result from making a sale.

Notice how good it feels when you choose an even bigger thought, such as:

I like the idea that I sell more than I expect today.

The key to choosing and replacing negative thoughts with positive ones is that your new thoughts MUST be believable.

What's wonderful about Powerful Thinking on Purpose is that the more you practice, the better you'll feel. The better you feel, the more you practice, and the easier it becomes. It's human nature to get better with practice.

With each new thought, you are creating new neural pathways in your mind. The more you practice Powerful Thinking on Purpose, the more you are reinforcing these neural pathways so that your subconscious mind begins to think this way naturally, without prompting.

Chapter 2

The Secret Garden in Your Mind

Your Conscious Mind

There are two distinct parts of your mind: your subconscious mind and your conscious mind. Your conscious mind is the part of you that is responsible for logic and reason. If I asked you to tell me what two plus two equals, or how to delete a file in your computer, you would come up with the answer by using your conscious mind.

Your conscious mind is that part of you that is in charge of your daily analytical and critical thinking. It contains only what you are focusing on that moment. It's the part of you that can operate computers, read books, and handle day-to-day tasks. Judgment and choice both arise from your conscious mind. You use your conscious mind to make thousands of daily decisions.

Scientists have been studying the conscious and subconscious mind for decades. It's no surprise that this is one area of science that continues to be challenging to research. Scientists generally agree that the conscious mind, in any given moment, holds only a small amount of information. According to Nelson Cowan[*], our conscious mind's working capacity to hold information is limited to a mere three or four items.

Your Subconscious Mind

On the other side, your subconscious mind contains everything. This part of your mind holds all your memories, experiences, emotions, and also your imagination. Everything you have heard, seen, felt, tasted, touched, smelled, and experienced in your life is stored here and can be accessed faster than you can blink.

Three important facts about your subconscious mind are:

1. **Your subconscious mind holds all of your feelings and emotions.**
2. **Your imagination resides in your subconscious mind.**
3. **Everything you have experienced is held in your subconscious mind.**

---

[*] The Magical Number 4 in Short-Term Memory: A Reconsideration of Mental Storage Capacity, Behavioral and Brain Sciences, Vol. 24, No. 1, pages 87-114, Feb. 2001

Here is where things get tricky: Your subconscious mind is the part that is designed to protect you and is always in control. Your subconscious mind is also the part that always wins.

When you hold negative thoughts and worries in your conscious mind, your subconscious mind believes that this is how you want to feel. It will do everything in its power to make sure that you get what it thinks you want. Because it thinks that you really want to feel anxious and worried, it will make sure that this happens. Ultimately your life reflects your thoughts. Your outer experience mirrors what your inner thoughts create.

If you ever wonder what your thoughts have been, take an honest look at your life right now. Your life reflects your thoughts and beliefs as they are held in your mind.

"Our minds become magnetized with the dominating thoughts we hold in our minds and these magnets attract to us the forces, the people, the circumstances of life which harmonize with the nature of our dominating thoughts."

-Napoleon Hill

All of your beliefs, experiences, and expectations are stored in your subconscious mind. Your subconscious mind holds a vast amount of information and it generates your emotional responses based on its experiences. This is the part of your mind where you have the ability to make profound and lasting changes.

Ever wonder why some people scream immediately when they see a spider or a mouse? Their subconscious mind is reacting to an old thought, belief, or fear. In reality, if that person would use their conscious mind to think analytically, he might realize that a mouse, much weaker and smaller than a human, really cannot do him any harm. When you react, you are always reacting with your subconscious mind, not your logical, analytical conscious mind.

I like to explain to clients that their subconscious mind has no opinions and is just like a garden. The ground in your garden has no opinions either.

Imagine you're preparing to plant some Forget-Me-Not flower seeds in the corner of your garden. You thoughtfully choose the perfect location to plant them, use your shovel to prepare the soil, and drop the seeds in the ground. You carefully cover the seeds with dirt and take time to regularly water the new seeds.

While you were planting, not once did the ground in your garden ever say to you:

Hey, are you SURE you want those blue flowers over there? It's really not a good place for them. They will grow much better over there under that large tree. And I've got to let you know that these are going to become little blue flowers and your favorite color is pink. Are you sure this what you really want?

Of course your garden will never utter a word. Your garden will simply accept the seeds, nurture them and allow the seeds to take root and to grow. The ground in your garden voices no opinions the same way your subconscious mind has no opinions.

After planting your seeds, you water your Forget-Me-Nots frequently and the roots begin to grow deeper. These pretty little blue flowers begin to sprout and grow larger. You know that whatever you plant and water in your garden, whether seeds or flowers or bushes or trees, will begin to grow. Some plants grow quickly. Others may take longer.

So what does this have to do with your subconscious mind? When you were young, your mind was very much like this garden. Thoughts, ideas, and beliefs took seed in your garden every day. And like a garden accepting a plant, your mind accepted many beliefs without question. Your mind never responded by replying:

Are you SURE you want to believe this?

In my practice, I frequently help people who want to overcome their fears. Not surprisingly, I've noticed that most fears took root in their subconscious mind at an early age.

When you are young and internalize a new belief, no matter how outlandish or unfounded, or where it came from, your subconscious mind unquestionably accepts this new belief as truth.

And unless something happens to change it, this belief will remain in your subconscious mind for years or even decades.

Your subconscious mind is an extremely important part of you because it stores your imagination, thoughts, and feelings. You wouldn't be who you are if you didn't have a subconscious mind. It is also a fierce protector. If you want to do something that is in conflict with your subconscious beliefs, your subconscious will do everything in its power to make sure it won't happen. In Chapter 12, Your Personal Protector, you'll learn how your subconscious mind sometimes stops you from doing what you want.

DID YOU KNOW?

The same way that plants and flowers attract birds, bees, butterflies, and insects, the thoughts in your mind attract things.

Negative thoughts tend to attract negative situations, causing unhappiness and misery.

Positive thoughts tend to attract opportunities, possibilities, comfort, and happiness.

Chapter 3

5 Powerful Words

Changing My Reality

When I was younger, I was just about the most negative person you could imagine. I was so negative and unhappy that if I could have separated from myself, I would have.

On any given day I had perhaps two positive thoughts. OK, that may be a bit of an exaggeration, but rarely were 10 percent of my thoughts positive. Some weeks, the only upbeat thought I could muster was "Well, at least my TV works."

Over time, I learned the techniques detailed in this book. Because I have learned to control and direct my thoughts, I would estimate that now over 90 percent of my thoughts are positive. The old negative ones still slip in occasionally, though. What's different is that now I know how to change these negative thoughts; they don't hang around as long as they used to.

When I was younger, I was aware that most people were happier than me. It wasn't hard to tell that the people who thought positively were more content and appeared to have fulfilling lives. Or maybe the people who were content and had fulfilling lives seemed happier. No matter what the cause, I wanted to feel better and become happier.

For some reason though, it was really hard for me to feel happy or positive. Frankly, the reason I failed was because I was unable to believe I could feel good about my life. I believed that life wasn't fair.

Life was tough for me and I believed that things would always continue to be difficult. This was my reality. Not a great place to hang out.

Deep inside, I knew instinctively that if I could think in a different way, things might change. I could feel better. So I tried hard to think differently.

I tried to pretend I was happy.

I tried to smile a lot.

I tried to feel good.

It was awful because the more I tried different ways of feeling good and being positive, the more frustrated and unhappy I became.

One day, in an effort to feel better, I said this sentence to myself:

I am happy.

Immediately my inner mind retorted:

No you're not. That's a load of crap.

Then I said to myself:

I want to be happy.

My inner voice responded quickly with a snarl:

Well then, keep on wanting. Maybe when pigs fly it will happen.

Then, in a huff of frustration I said to myself:

I LIKE the idea that I can be happy.

And I waited.

And waited some more. I heard nothing from my inner mind. It finally had nothing to refute. It was definitely a weird moment. I knew something was different. Maybe I accepted that statement as truth?

So I decided to continue to say that to myself over and over. For days, I repeated this sentence to myself.

Then I noticed a profound change. The thought:

I like the idea that I can be happy.

had somehow taken root in my mind. I noticed tiny pockets of time when I truly DID feel happy. Nothing huge or earth shattering. I wasn't 100 percent top-of-the-world ecstatic, but I was aware that I occasionally felt better.

Somehow, the way I worded this statement was so different that my subconscious mind accepted it much more easily. I realized that had stumbled upon something. The words:

I like the idea that...

caused my statement to feel true for me.

I realized that if I really wanted to make a change, that adding these 5 Powerful Words to my statement caused me to believe it wholly. Rewording it caused it to become a thought that didn't meet with resistance. I was amazed that this new, believable thought was so easily accepted into my subconscious mind without any resistance.

Trying It Out With a Client

When I am with my clients, I see our relationship as a partnership. I do my part and it's important for my client to do his or her part by reinforcing new thoughts and feelings. Clients do this by repeating their powerful personal statement and combining it with an appropriate visualization. You'll learn this technique in Chapter 13.

After a coaching session focused on increasing sales confidence for an employee benefits insurance executive, I asked my client to reinforce his session with this personal statement:

I easily reach my sales goals.

I asked him to say this to himself and report to me on a scale of 0 to 100 percent how believable this statement was for him.

He said:

"About 75 percent. But I really DO want this to be the truth."

OK, I thought. We're close, but not quite there. So instead of him repeating:

I easily reach my sales goals.

I asked my client to repeat this new statement and tell me how it feels and how believable it is:

I like the idea that I easily reach my sales goals.

He repeated it and smiled saying:

"It's 100 percent believable!"

Using the phrase "I like the idea that" made a tremendous difference with this client. He was able to believe his powerful personal statement. At his next appointment he said he felt great and had a great week. He asked:

"After a few days I began to drop off the 'I like the idea that.' Is this okay?"

His question to me was proof that his subconscious mind accepted his new, powerful personal statement and when he had internalized it, he naturally shortened it. He no longer had to *"like the idea"* because he really felt that he could reach his sales goals.

It may be hard to believe, but after the first session it's typical that clients become more aware of their thoughts. They also notice the difference in their feelings when they take control of their thoughts. I've noticed, though, that many have a lingering subconscious concern. A part of them may have a worry or fear that they might not succeed, but of course, they aren't aware of this.

My goal is to help my clients create new thoughts and beliefs so they can achieve their goals without struggling. Any resistance to a new thought will ultimately cause people to give up. I want to bypass any subconscious resistance to their new statement. I want to make sure that what clients are repeating to themselves is believable.

When a thought is 100 percent believable, then change can occur without resistance.

As a result of my experience with my client, I realized that I was onto something. I knew I had discovered a new way of phrasing powerful personal statements. I had discovered an efficient and simple way of permitting the subconscious mind to begin to accept a new change without resistance.

I began sharing this with more and more clients and I noticed that they were feeling better and experiencing benefits much more rapidly.

Adding the 5 Powerful Words to their personal statement made it easier for them to stay on track with their goals. They were achieving their goals with less stress.

And all it took was the addition of 5 Powerful Words:

I like the idea that....

I was delighted.

DID YOU KNOW?

Your powerful personal statement is the secret key to your success.

It's a statement that you say to yourself that describes what you want to feel, have, or experience.

Chapter 4

Every Day in Every Way

It's human nature to want to be successful and so we like to seek help from those who have already achieved success. The first caveman helped his fellow man find shelter and food. These cavemen shared their knowledge about the land and, over time, taught others the benefits of fire for warmth and cooking.

As the number of people grew, we found more ways to help others. Early healers provided relief to their fellow man, from physical pain, hunger, and more. Physical healing was primary but, over time, early people began to help each other with emotional healing too.

Throughout history we've learned many techniques for physical and emotional healing. Reciting, listening, and writing affirmations are powerful techniques that have existed for thousands of years.

As long ago as 2000 years, the Egyptians used affirmations and healing suggestions in their sleep temples for the purpose of healing the mind and body.

While sleep temples are no longer around, they have been replaced by modern medicine and psychology. Today, many people's first choice is to take a pill to feel emotionally better.

As each generation discovers and learns the power of thought, they pass this powerful information to the next generation. Through word of mouth, books, movies, the internet, and more, many people now know that what we think has a direct effect on what we feel.

Émile Coué, The Father of Autosuggestion

If you were born at the turn of the 20th century, you might have heard of a powerful self-help technique that was popularized by Émile Coué, a charismatic pharmacist and psychologist from France.

A commonly held belief at that time was that a strong, persistent willpower constituted the best path to success. Coué maintained that curing some of our troubles required a change in our subconscious thought. Only after we change our subconscious thoughts, can we place ourselves on the path to personal success.

While Coué was working as a pharmacist, he noticed that he could improve the efficiency of a medication by praising its effectiveness to his patients. He became aware that the patients for whom he praised the medication had a noticeable improvement when compared to the patients who simply received their medication without a suggestion.

While Coué believed in medication, he observed that his patients could heal themselves more efficiently by replacing a "thought of illness" with "a thought of cure." At the time, it was a profound and unusual concept.

Coué believed that the repetition of words and images, once accepted by the subconscious mind, had the ability to heal both emotionally and physically. He believed that what you think tended to become true for you. He realized that if one of his clients had been ill and still believed he was ill, then he would remain ill. Of course, he may not have been the first to realize this, but he was certainly one of the first to popularize the benefits of positive thinking and positive self-talk.

Coué writes in his book:

Autosuggestion is as old as the hills; only we had forgotten to practice it and so we needed to learn it all over again. The power of thought, of idea, is ... immeasurable.

The world is dominated by thought. The human being individually is also entirely governed by his own thoughts, good or bad. The powerful action of the mind over the body which explains the effects of suggestion, was well known to the great thinkers of the Middle Ages, whose vigorous intelligence embraced the sum of human knowledge.

-Émile Coué, My Method and Self Mastery Through Conscious Autosuggestion, 1922

Émile Coué coined the phrase *"Every day in every way I'm getting better and better."* He instructed his patients to repeat this phrase throughout the day and to intentionally change their negative thoughts to positive thoughts.

When Coué arrived in the United States in 1923, he became so popular that a song was written by the famous Broadway duo, William Jerome and Jean Schwartz, and published by Jerome H. Remick & Co., NY. Copies of "Every Day in Every Way I'm Getting Better and Better, The Healthy Song" found their way to pianos in saloons and parlors across the country.

Here's the chorus for this popular song:

Day by day…in every way…
   I'm getting better and better every day!

On cloudy days this mental exercise
   will brighten up your eyes and bring you sunny skies…

Day by day…in every way…
   it's surely easy, and not so hard to say…

Learn this simple-ist of rhymes and repeat it twenty times…
   day by day I'm getting better every day!

Regarding the autosuggestion, "Every day in every way I'm getting better and better," famous singer and songwriter Johnny Cash remarked, "I didn't especially believe that about myself, but I said it every day and I made myself believe it and it worked. I never gave up my dream to sing on the radio. And that dream came true in 1955."

Chapter 5

What's Your Goal?

In order to achieve success, it's logical that the first thing you must have in mind is a specific goal.

Every goal begins with a thought. To achieve success, your goal must be in total alignment with your beliefs and desires. It's not enough to have a goal of something you want to do, be, or have. First and foremost, your goal must be *reasonable and believable* to you. This is crucial to your success.

If your dream is to be the captain of a National Basketball Association (NBA) team and you are 5 foot one inch tall and hate dribbling basketballs, then your goal isn't very reasonable or believable, is it?

On the other hand, if your goal is to be the Director of Marketing of an NBA team and you enjoy the challenges of marketing, then of course it's reasonable and believable.

Years ago, a famous film actor decided to go into politics. He had no prior political experience at all. But in his heart, he felt that his goal was reasonable and believable. If he had thought to himself, *"No actor has ever become a governor, therefore I will never get elected,"* how far do you think he would have gone? Most likely, his negative thought would have stopped him right then and there. Ronald Reagan clearly never had this thought. He kept his goals in mind to ultimately become Governor of California and the first actor elected as President of the United States.

NOW YOU KNOW

When you are in control of your thoughts, you are in control of your life.

It's important to be aware of your negative thoughts because they may get in the way of achieving your goals and desires. When you use the worksheets at the back of this book, you'll be on your way to bypassing those negative thoughts so you can achieve your goals.

Set Your Personal Goal

Think about some of the personal goals that you have set for yourself. Perhaps one of your goals is to lose weight. You might have other long-term goals, such as learning a new skill, going on vacation, buying a house, making more money, finding your soul mate, writing a book, or changing your career.

Short-term goals might be cleaning your home, exercising for twenty minutes daily, completing an assignment, or organizing your workspace.

Take a moment and think about what makes you feel happy and fulfilled in life. This can help you solidify your various goals.

Start with Small Steps

Sometimes personal goals are so big that they may feel unattainable. For example, if I want to become a news anchor and I try to imagine seeing myself on TV, I might find that it's such an unbelievable thought that I may eventually drop my dream. A more realistic way to achieve my goal is to break it down into smaller goals. For example, I could begin by visualizing myself interning during evenings or weekends in a local newsroom, or completing my first reporting assignment.

Most people tend to do much better when they take small steps towards their goals. This reminds me of a joke my brother told me when he was seven: "How do you eat an elephant? {Answer:} One bite at a time!"

With each small step, you can easily achieve some success. And when you have achieved a little success, it's easier to reach the next step, and the next step. Success enables more success. As you work through the sheets in the Appendix, you'll see how easy it is for you to take the next small step in your life to achieve your goal.

Achieving success, even with something small, is terrific. Each success adds to the one before, and the more successes you experience, the more your confidence increases. When you are confident, you automatically increase your potential for success.

Think about the time you learned how to ride a bike. Perhaps you began by learning on a tricycle. You put your feet on the pedals and learned that you could power your own bike. You could even turn the handles and, like magic, your tricycle went in the direction you chose. You achieved success! You learned how to be in control of your tricycle.

When you felt confident, you moved up to a bicycle with training wheels. You planted yourself firmly on the seat and smiled, feeling proud of yourself for being on a big bike... looking at the world from above, a few feet above the ground. What fun!

As your confidence increased, you were ready to take the next big step. It was time to ride your bike without training wheels. The training wheels were taken off and you hopped on top of your bike. Keeping one foot on the ground and the other on the pedal, you knew that you were ready.

As you held onto the handlebars, you pushed down on the pedal. Then, you took a breath and placed your other foot on the pedal. You felt that wonderful feeling as your bicycle wheels moved forward and all of a sudden, you were riding all on your own. What an exhilarating feeling!

Ask yourself, how hard would it be to learn to ride if you had to get on a regular bike without the experience of a tricycle and training wheels? Would success be as easy? Of course not.

It's important to remember to take it easy on yourself and start with small, believable steps.

SUCCESS STORY

*Comedian Jim Carrey has long told the story of his rise to fame. One of the most interesting stories Carrey has shared is the fact that well before he was rich and famous, he wrote a check to himself in the amount of 10 million dollars for "acting services rendered". He postdated the check for 1995 and carried it in his wallet. Carrey also visualized himself cashing the check and what he would buy with it. By the time 1995 rolled around, Jim Carrey was indeed wealthy enough to cash the check (according to the book **Jim Carrey** by Amy Stone, he never cashed it; Carrey instead put the check in his father's coat pocket after he passed away, as a symbol of his father's dreams and support for his son's success).*

Putting your goal on paper is the first step to achieving it.

Putting it on paper makes it real.

Write three personal goals (short-term or long-term) below:

My goal is_____.

My goal is_____.

My goal is_____.

Chapter 6

Custom Made to Fit Every Time

Perhaps you are fed up with where you are and desire a better life. Maybe you are tired of meeting people who aren't right for you. You might feel frustrated with where you are in your career, or even feel stuck and not know how to make a change.

You go out and buy a book that promises that your life will change. You read the book and are thrilled that the author has experienced amazing and wonderful changes by using affirmations. You may begin to experience excitement because you now feel you have the potential to change, just as the author has. After reading and studying the book in detail, you decide to go for it.

You know you are as capable as the next person. You know that others have achieved personal success and they are no better or worse than you. You deserve to live your dream life.

You have now completed the book and conscientiously followed the author's suggestions to read the affirmations daily. You don't skip a day. Every day you wake up and read or recite the affirmations. You repeat them on the way to work and even in the shower. Every night before you go to bed, you read and repeat the affirmations again.

After a few weeks of dutifully repeating the affirmations night and day, you wake up and notice that NOTHING has changed.

You notice that you feel the same way you did when you first purchased the book. You are living the same old life. You are your same old self. You are hearing the same old repetitive thoughts in your mind. You haven't attracted your perfect partner. You have the same job. Those same old habits control you. The promised miracle hasn't occurred.

You feel discouraged and disheartened. Why do affirmations seem to work for other people and not for you? Did you do something wrong? Maybe you begin to feel you don't deserve to have what you want in life. You sadly realize that reading, writing, and spending so much time on those affirmations didn't make a bit of difference.

You decide to throw out anything to do with affirmations and look for another way to improve your life.

But wait! Don't give up!

You didn't do anything wrong. There is a reason your life didn't change. There is a simple explanation for what went wrong. As you begin to recognize and learn the secrets of Powerful Thinking on Purpose, you will find that it *really is easy* to improve your life.

But I Don't Believe It

The reason that most affirmations fail is that most people hold a belief in their subconscious mind that prevents the affirmation from being accepted.

When you say an affirmation to yourself, such as:

I will make three hundred thousand dollars this year.

and your first thought is:

I like this idea, but...

or

I don't think this is really possible...

I guarantee that you'll never achieve your goal.

In the following chapters you'll learn the elements needed to create your own powerful personal statements that work. At the same time you'll be guided to focus on those steps that you need to achieve your goals.

The Importance of Customization

It's your life and only your personal statements will work for you.
Affirmations written by someone else won't work for you.
Your teacher's affirmations won't work for you; your neighbor's won't work for you. The simple secret is that only yours
will work for you.

SUCCESS STORY

*One of my goals was to become my own boss. I had
never worked for myself, and was scared stiff, but
knew I couldn't keep going on with someone else
pulling my strings. I said daily affirmations: "I
am so happy and grateful that I am my own boss
working from my home office." I said it, wrote it
and prayed it...and guess what? I am now my
own boss working from my home office!!! I also
did the same thing to get my dream house when
I didn't even have any money for the down pay-
ment. I am now living in my dream house that
I own, with every detail that I envisioned and
affirmed.*

-*Marla Martenson, Author, Dating Coach*

Even though affirmations often don't work, Marla's worked for
her because they were personalized and followed the same for-
mat as the rules you are learning right now.

Making your statements personal is an important part of positive change. You'll get a much greater reward when you learn
how to create your own rather than using someone else's. Your
powerful personal statement will work much more rapidly

because you can customize it to bypass any personal (and sub-conscious) resistance that you might be holding onto.

What I mean by resistance is really any personal thoughts or beliefs that may get in the way of achieving your desires. I'll be talking about this later in more detail in Chapter 10, Getting Stuck by Limiting Beliefs. The important thing to remember now is that YOUR powerful personal statement will always fit YOU quite well. It won't, however, fit your friends or your neighbors as well as it will fit you.

Powerful personal statements are just like retainers for your teeth made by the orthodontist. When you use someone else's affirmations, it's like wearing someone else's retainers. They were not molded to fit your mouth and eventually you'll discard them because they don't feel right.

For your personal success, you need to create and use your own statements. Just as only your retainers will fit you perfectly, your powerful personal statements need to fit too.

Now that you know this secret, just imagine all the changes you can make to improve your life. You can attract more money, you can have a job that you enjoy, and you can even find a partner who is perfect for you. Read on and you'll learn how you can *easily create* powerful personal statements that will work for you.

Chapter 7

Choose to have a
great day

Powerful Personal Statements - Success Starts Here

A carefully worded and well-formed personal statement is the key to aligning your thoughts and feelings with your desires and goals. A powerful personal statement is simply a thought that you will use to intentionally improve your life.

You will be repeating your personal statement to help you stay on track and achieve your goal without struggling. A custom, well-thought-out sentence will enable you to create new thoughts, beliefs, and behaviors to help you reach your goals *without struggling.*

In the upcoming chapters, you will learn how to use your personal statement to easily stay on target by keeping you focused on what you want. Focusing on your desires will eliminate the strain and stress that result from always focusing on negative outcomes. Focusing on what you want will ultimately help you to enjoy the journey while you are reaching your goal.

In the Appendix of this book, you'll find your personal worksheets. Completing your worksheets will help you to clarify your goals and thoughts. Once you use them, you'll begin to integrate the concepts and you'll start to notice when you are faced with personal resistance. Your worksheets will help you to create powerful statements that are specific to you, so that you can reach your goal while feeling great and more optimistic.

As a National Guild of Hypnotists Certified Instructor, I teach the process of writing powerful personal statements to all my students. As a High Performance U Coach, I also teach my clients to use powerful statements every day to help them achieve their personal and professional goals.

It's important that each client reinforces the thought and habit changes they desire, or they risk slipping back into old, unwanted patterns. They don't have to do this for months or years. It's only needed until their new thoughts, beliefs, and habits are in alignment with their goals.

When new clients come to me for the first time, they learn that what I do to help them doesn't come in the form of a "magic pill" (though it does sometimes seem to appear this way). Clients learn that reinforcement using powerful personal statements is a *key* component to personal thought change and success.

As you learn and incorporate Powerful Thinking on Purpose into your life, you may notice how quickly it becomes second nature to you. You'll automatically begin to be aware of your thoughts and remember to reinforce new habits and belief changes by repeating your personal statement.

Choose To Have A Great Day

What you think about and what you focus on is what you attract in your life. If you discover only one thing from reading this book, this is the most important concept. You always have a choice about which thoughts you keep. You can continue to think about "what is" (i.e. my life is miserable, nothing good ever happens), or you can choose to think about what you want and how you want to live your life.

When you wake up in the morning and think and grumble about how unhappy you are and that nothing good ever happens, then most likely you will continue to be unhappy for the day.

When you wake up in the morning and decide to say to yourself:

I choose to have a great day today.

then you have a better chance of having a great day. Using your thoughts in a purposeful way will get you where you want to go.

Here's an easy way to show yourself that your thoughts have power. Every morning for the next 30 days, as soon as you wake up, choose to tell yourself that you want to have a wonderful day. Repeat the following sentence in your mind or out loud 10 times each morning:

I like the idea that I will have a wonderful day today.

Then take a moment and imagine yourself at the end of the day smiling and feeling great. It's OK if you don't believe that you'll feel any better. Just give it a try. I guarantee that the more you do this, the more you'll notice that you feel much more positive when you check in with yourself at the end of each day.

In only a few days, you will most likely notice a difference in your life. Perhaps something amazing has happened. Something you didn't expect. Or maybe you notice that your outlook or attitude has improved. With just this one exercise, you will have jump-started yourself on the path to achieving your goals.

The most important and valuable skill you can develop is that of intentionally directing your thoughts. Throughout the day you'll have thousands of thoughts. Persistent thoughts of worry, anxiety, and fear will cause you undue stress. Your goal is to notice when you are having these negative thoughts and consciously answer the question

How do I want to feel right now?

By answering this question you will feel more optimistic as your thoughts and feelings begin to focus on what you want.

Chapter 8

Staying Calm in an Uncertain World

According to Dr. Andrew Weil, stress can cause a multitude of problems. On his web site (http://www.drweil.com), Dr. Weil outlines some staggering facts about how stress can affect our lives:

1. **Stress has been linked** to all the leading causes of death, such as cardiovascular disease, cancer, and suicide.

2. **Almost 90 percent** of all visits to primary health care providers are due to stress-related problems.

3. **Nearly one-half** of all adults suffer adverse effects from stress.

It is estimated that one million Americans miss work due to stress-related complaints.

Learning how to change the way you talk to yourself in the midst of stressful situations can help you stay healthy and remain calm.

When I was pregnant with my first child, I found myself becoming extremely stressed every time I watched the news. I was now looking at life from a different viewpoint. Knowing that I was going to be responsible for my child and realizing that I had no control over what was going on in the world caused a huge amount of my stress.

At that time another war was in full swing. There was a frightening measles outbreak in the city. We were expecting the worst winter of the decade. Taxes were going up. The economy needed major repairs. Our health system was a mess. Sound familiar? These were the headlines in 1990.

Not much has changed. Unfortunately, these are the same types of headlines that have bombarded us for decades.

I spent way too much time worrying and stressing about things that I had no control over. Not a rewarding hobby.

Do you ever worry about things that you have no control over? If you don't, then skip to the next chapter. If you do, I'm going to share a simple way to reduce your worry. Before I do that, consider this fact:

A fear or worry is a thought about something that hasn't happened yet

You can worry about something bad that might happen. And while you are worrying, you are causing yourself stress. When whatever it is you are worrying about doesn't happen, you will have spent a lot of time feeling stressed. If it does happen, you still will have spent a lot of time feeling stressed.

Wouldn't it be great if worrying could cause something wonderful to happen? It's a shame that it doesn't work this way, especially because we spend so much energy and time worrying. But worrying can't change anything. Only action results in change.

If stress and worry are useful feelings that cause you to take positive action, that's fine. Once you take the action you need, is continued worrying necessary?

If you are not in a position to take action, then why worry? Worrying without action is simply a waste of your good energy that can be used in a more helpful way.

Below are some typical issues that we tend to worry about. Underneath each thought is a sample sentence you can say to yourself every time you catch yourself worrying.

After you begin substituting your new sentence, you'll start to notice how much better you feel. The better you feel, the more you'll want to incorporate these new sentences and thoughts into your everyday thinking.

INSTRUCTIONS: The moment you notice you are worrying, immediately:

1. Ask yourself, "How do I want to feel?"
2. Then start your new positive sentence with the words: *I like the idea that...*

EXAMPLES

I'm worried that the economy will get worse.

I like the idea that everything works out OK.

I'm worried that I will get sick.

I like the idea that I am healthy and fine.

I'm worried that the stock market will go down.

I like the idea that I am invested well and I feel relaxed.

I'm worried that I'll get lost.

I like the idea that I find my way.

I'm worried that I'll get laid off.

I like the idea that everything works out fine.

I'm worried we'll have a blizzard.

I like the idea that our power stays on and we are fine.

The phrase, *I like the idea that* will force you to:

1. Focus on what you want and
2. Reduce your stress.

The more you use this phrase, the better you'll feel. It's amazing what the 5 Powerful Words, *I like the idea that,* can do.

Take a moment to do the following short exercise to show yourself how easy it is to feel better when you change your self-talk.

QUICK EXERCISE

Ask yourself, *"What is my biggest worry right now?"*

Example: *"I am worried that I will lose my job."*

Fill in the blank:

I am worried that_____.

Read the above sentence and answer the following questions using the scale below:

0% - -10 - - 20 - -30 - - 40 - - 50 - - 60 - - 70 - - 80 - - 90 - - 100%

Not Possible---Possible

    1. What is the possibility of this occurring?
I believe that there is a_____% chance of this occurring.

    2. Now write the opposite of your worry statement:

Example: *"I am calm and secure in my job."*

or *"I can always find a way to make money."*

Fill in the blank:

I am_____.

    3. Read the above sentence and answer the following question using the scale below:

0% - -10 - - 20 - -30 - - 40 - - 50 - - 60 - - 70 - - 80 - - 90 - - 100%

Not Possible-- Possible

What is the possibility of this occurring?

I believe that there is a_____% chance of this occurring.

Did you notice that both sentences you wrote, whether positive or negative, stated something that is possible?

It's interesting that most of the time, we tend to focus on the negative thought, even when there is the possibility that the outcome can be positive.

Which thought feels better to you? The negative thought or the positive thought?

Rewrite your positive thought here:

I am_____.

Ask yourself: *"How much do I believe this?"*

If you don't believe your positive thought 100 percent,

then rewrite it here:

I like the idea that_____.

Ask yourself: *"How much do I believe this thought now?"*

By adding the five words, "I like the idea that," you have increased your belief in this thought.

Now that you have completed this simple exercise, you can see how easy it is to create a new, believable, powerful statement. For the next twenty-four hours, take the time to intentionally notice your thoughts. When they are heading into that negative territory do the following:

1. Ask yourself: "How do I want to feel?"
2. Then start your new positive sentence with the words: *I like the idea that...*

You'll be pleasantly surprised when you find that you have easily reduced your stress with this simple exercise.

NOW YOU KNOW

A well-formed powerful personal statement is an effective tool that you can use any time you want to feel good about something you have no control over. You can also use it when you want to reach a personal goal without struggling.

Chapter 9

How Does Powerful Thinking on Purpose Work?

When you are stuck with old thoughts that are holding you back, it's almost impossible to take action to achieve your goals.

Powerful personal statements are thoughts you choose on purpose that are designed to take root directly in your subconscious mind. Remember that your subconscious mind is the one that is in charge of your emotions and feelings.

New beliefs are formed when a correctly worded powerful thought is accepted into your subconscious mind. This new belief then directly affects your attitude and ultimately your actions. As your attitude changes and you become open to possibilities, it then becomes easy to take action.

When you repeat and internalize your powerful personal statement, you are actively creating positive changes in your subconscious mind. You have the ability to use your powerful statements to reprogram your mind, eliminate old emotional triggers, and respond to situations in a different way.

One way to understand this is that your thoughts have a direct affect on your beliefs. Your beliefs affect your attitude.

And your attitude has a direct affect on your actions.

THOUGHTS ➜ BELIEF

BELIEF ➜ ATTITUDE

ATTITUDE ➜ ACTION

Taking action is necessary for life changes to occur. Without action, nothing happens. Without action, everything remains the same.

Another way to look at this is that first you **think**. Your thoughts cause you to **feel** a particular way. Your feelings affect what you **do** in your life. And what you do directly corresponds to what happens in your life.

"The ancestor of every action is a thought."

-Ralph Waldo Emerson

Let's say, for example, that you want to lose weight but it has always been a struggle for you. One aspect of losing weight means that you have to give up things that you enjoy, like chocolate. You know that you might not have to eliminate chocolate forever, but you are concerned that if you allowed yourself to even have a small amount of chocolate right now, it might lead to eating more.

As you think more about this, instead of eliminating chocolate, you decide that you would rather be in control of how much chocolate you eat.

So you choose to do something different, and intentionally create a clear goal of limiting yourself to 50 calories of chocolate per day. You tell yourself that you want to feel content with 50 calories of chocolate; even though you aren't sure you will ever be satisfied with such a small amount. You really like the idea of never feeling deprived while you lose weight.

Deep down, though, you are worried that this won't work. You are concerned that you won't be able to stay on track and limit yourself to only 50 calories.

Here's where your personal statement will make *all* the difference in the world. You want to create a powerful personal statement that will help you to change your thoughts and make it easier for you to achieve your goal. You want to feel satisfied with 50 calories of chocolate and you don't want to feel compelled to eat more. Every time you think about or eat chocolate, you want it to be in your control.

To help you reach your goal, you create a personal statement that is true for you and that will lead you to easily shift your thoughts and eating habits about chocolate.

Try the sentence below:

I eat 50 calories of chocolate every day and I feel satisfied.

Now look at that sentence. Read it again. Think about it. Does it feel true and believable? Did you notice a resounding "yes!" in your mind? In my experience only a small percentage of people will find that it is completely 100 percent believable. Most people probably won't believe it. If you are in the latter group, you might notice that something doesn't feel quite right about that sentence. *But you'd like it to be absolutely true!*

Perhaps you feel as if you are lying to yourself when you say that sentence. Not a big lie. Just a little tiny one. The more you think about it, you know deep inside of you that it doesn't ring true. It's almost like saying:

I'm going to be satisfied eating 15 M&M's.

(Who am I kidding? Satisfied?)

You might even think:

No way. Most likely I'll feel really deprived.

No way is this statement true for me.

The sentence:

I eat 50 calories of chocolate and I feel satisfied.

may not be in line with your thoughts and feelings. It might not feel true and right for you. When a sentence like this doesn't feel true, there is no way you can use it to help you reach a goal.

For a sentence to work for you, it must be congruent with your personal beliefs. It must feel right for you. When it is, it becomes your powerful personal statement. If your subconscious mind (where your beliefs reside) does not accept this sentence, then you are wasting your time. Your willpower will run out and you'll give up quickly because it's too stressful to continually say something to yourself that isn't true for you—no matter how much you want it to be true.

NOW YOU KNOW

When a correctly worded powerful personal statement is accepted into your subconscious mind, it becomes a thought that is believable.

Ultimately, your new believable thought directly affects your attitude. Your attitude has a direct affect upon your actions.

The purpose of a powerful personal statement is to help you take action to achieve your desire: it might be to lose weight, get rid of the fear of speaking in public, increase your sales, attract a partner, start a business, eliminate a bad habit, or even improve sports performance.

Of course, simply reading a positive statement will not cause you to take immediate action of any sort. It is, however, the first step toward helping yourself create a new, beneficial belief in your subconscious mind.

When you use your powerful personal statement, you aren't going to be simply repeating words to yourself. Nor will you be sitting quietly and wishing for what you want. You'll be "kicking it up a few notches" by combining your personal statement with power ingredients that you'll learn later on in the book. You will be repeating your powerful statement while you use your imagination to feel and experience your goal *in a new way.*

I Really Want This!

You can want something and at the same time you might not believe that it's possible for you to achieve it.

There is a huge difference between wanting something and *feeling, imagining, and knowing* that it is possible to attain.

Let's explore this concept. Maybe you really want to make a lot of money. Perhaps you've been thinking about this for a long time. You dream of how you will spend your money. You think about the places you will travel—free of any worries about finances. You may even imagine what it feels like to live in your perfect home and drive a shiny new luxury car. At your very core you know you really want to have a huge amount of money.

TAKE A MOMENT FOR YOURSELF NOW:

Write down a few things that you want. Maybe you want more money. Maybe you want the perfect relationship. Maybe you want to lose weight.

For example it might be, "I really want to be the top salesperson this year," or "I really want to own a summer home."

*1. I really want*_____.

*2. I really want*_____.

*3. I really want*_____.

After you have filled in the spaces above, rewrite #1 in the space below. Now, out loud, read the sentence below emphasizing the word "really."

"I *really* want _____."

Now, say it out loud three more times. Notice your thoughts and feelings while you repeat these words. While you are speaking, ask yourself:

"Do I believe 100 percent to my very core that I WANT this?"

Make sure that your answer to this question is a simple "Yes" or "No." Put your attention on your thoughts and feelings while you answer the question.

Next, read the second sentence and ask yourself, "Do I believe 100 percent to my very core that I want this?"

Finally, read the third sentence and ask yourself, "Do I believe 100 percent to my very core that I want this?"

Yes, But...

What were your thoughts and feelings when you answered these questions? Some of you might have answered with a resounding "Yes!" If you did, it's proof that your desires are congruent with your beliefs.

While answering the question above though, you may have noticed some internal thoughts and feelings. Perhaps you had a fleeting thought when you asked yourself if you believe 100 percent to your core that you want this. Or you might have noticed a small feeling that when translated sounds like "yeah, but…"

In a moment, you will discover how to listen to yourself to identify any blocks that may get in the way of achieving your goals and desires.

INSTRUCTIONS:

If you had a "yeah, but…" feeling, say the sentence five times and _immediately jot down whatever comes to your mind_ after the word "**but.**"

Whatever pops into your head goes on the lines below. Place no judgments on your thoughts. It doesn't matter if your thoughts feel odd, ridiculous, or unfounded.

I really want _____, but….

(write your sentence above)

Quickly write your responses below.

But_____

But_____

But_____

But_____

But_____

What did you notice? What thoughts came to your mind after the word "**But**"?

Some people's sentences might look like this:

*I want to make a million dollars, **but**....* <u>*I don't believe it will really happen.*</u>

*I want to make a million dollars, **but**....* <u>*no one in my family makes money.*</u>

*I want to make a million dollars, **but**....* <u>*my friends might be jealous.*</u>

*I want to make a million dollars, **but**....* <u>*I haven't done anything to deserve it.*</u>

*I want to make a million dollars, **but**....* <u>*it's not good to want lots of money.*</u>

All of the above are examples of limiting thoughts and beliefs. These are negative thoughts and beliefs that will be boulders on your path to your goals. Because of this, they are commonly labeled "limiting beliefs" or "limiting thoughts."

NOW YOU KNOW

For a powerful personal statement to work for you, it must feel TRUE for you. If it is not true, you can sense it. When you read it you'll notice a tiny voice that says, "yeah, but," or you'll notice a feeling inside that indicates it isn't true for you.

Chapter 10

Getting Stuck by Limiting Beliefs

You hold two different kinds of beliefs in your subconscious mind. One kind of belief can stop you from moving forward, while the other belief can empower you to reach amazing heights.

A "limiting belief" is a thought in your mind that can get in the way of you moving forward in your life and achieving your goals. It's a thought that may have been true for you at one time, but may not be true now, even though part of your mind still acts as though it's relevant.

Of course, it's not your conscious analytical mind that holds this belief. Limiting beliefs are always firmly planted somewhere in your subconscious mind. Limiting beliefs can cause you to struggle while you attempt to reach your goal. Your subconscious wants to make sure that what it believes and what you do are in alignment. When you want to achieve a goal and your subconscious doesn't believe it's possible, it will do its best to sabotage your success.

You might not know that there is a limiting belief somewhere in the back of your mind, but you might notice a *"yeah, but..."* feeling inside yourself.

When you happen to notice a limiting belief and it's in the tiniest little voice you hear for only a brief second, **pay attention to it!** Don't sweep it under the rug and hope it goes away. Your limiting belief is making itself known to you. This is a very valuable piece of information that can help you succeed in reaching your goals.

Limiting beliefs are a sign of personal inner resistance. You must address your own limiting belief in order to achieve success more easily. If you ignore it, it will most likely cause you to constantly struggle and feel stressed while you are trying to reach your goal.

Below are examples of limiting beliefs:

I'm not good enough.
Other people are better than me.
It's selfish of me to want more.
To be successful I have to give up my personal life.

Losing weight is hard work.
I'll never be thin.
I have to deprive myself to lose weight.
Money is the root of all evil.
People who make a lot of money are snobby.
If I make a lot of money, my friends will be jealous.
People who make a lot of money are selfish.

"What we can or cannot do, what we consider possible or impossible, is rarely a function of our true capability. It is more likely a function of our beliefs about who we are."

-ANTHONY ROBBINS

TAKE A MOMENT FOR YOURSELF NOW:

No matter how uncomfortable or silly your beliefs may be, it's important to pay attention to them. Limiting beliefs will always get in the way of your success. If you ignore them, you'll find yourself struggling to stay on your path. When you pay attention to them, you have the opportunity to transform or release them.

Take a moment to jot down the first thoughts that come into your mind when you read the following:

I'll never make a lot of money
because _____

_____

_____.

It's hard for me to lose weight

*because*_____

_____

_____ .

I'll never be as successful as I want

*because*_____

_____

_____ .

The sentences that you wrote above reveal that you have limiting beliefs getting in the way of your success. I don't know anyone who doesn't have some thoughts that have the possibility to hinder their personal success.

The big secret to personal success is recognizing and eliminating or changing these thoughts; when you do, you'll be well on your way to achieving success!

Knowing that you have thoughts that have been barriers on the path to your success is extremely useful information. Understanding this means that you can now work towards eliminating these thoughts.

You are now learning to use powerful personal statements to destroy these old limiting beliefs. At the same time, they smooth the path for your inner mind to accept your new positive beliefs.

By the way, there are other ways to get past resistance and achieve your goals. You can pray, use hypnosis, work with a therapist, tap on meridian points, and a myriad of other techniques. Use whatever works best for you.

You can use your powerful statements alone or combine them with other techniques that are helpful to you. In my experience, using powerful personal statements is simply the easiest, most cost effective, and logical way to shift your thoughts, beliefs, attitudes, and ultimately your personal actions.

"Everything you want is out there waiting for you to ask. Everything you want also wants you. But you have to take action to get it."

-JACK CANFIELD

While you are on the path to actively improve your life, you might notice that not everyone is interested in personal improvement. Some people might not want to be bothered with improving their lives. Others are quite comfortable with their personal issues and enjoy the drama they create. Lots of people don't even believe that they can make positive changes.

Many people also like the idea that hoping and wishing for what they want will be enough to reach their goals. This would be an easy way to get what they want. When you hope and wish, all you get is more hoping and wishing. But now, *you* know better.

NOW YOU KNOW

Old beliefs can prevent you from achieving your goals.

SUCCESS STORY

I'm a VP in the insurance industry. I have a high salary and in order to make a job change, I knew I'd have to make a huge financial sacrifice. After 24 years in the industry, I thought I was at the pinnacle of my career, but I was miserable. The daily stress was horrendous. I felt that there was no way out. To support my family, I felt that I was doomed to be stuck in this awful situation forever.

I never thought that changing jobs was possible for me; I had so many negative thoughts about why I couldn't leave. It didn't occur to me that these thoughts could be wrong.

A few months ago during the height of the recession, I said to myself "I need to leave this job. It's stressing me out, I'm angry and miserable. I'm in a bad situation, but I'm really afraid that if I leave this job I'll make a lot less money."

I had to find a solution for my stress...

Working with Wendy as a High Performance U Coach, I learned how my thoughts affect my attitudes and actions. She and I created a powerful personal statement. I repeated this consistently every morning and evening while imagining myself feeling great.

"I like the idea that I'm happy, fulfilled, and confident."

In less than two weeks of repeating my powerful personal statement, I had an epiphany. I knew that all those negative thoughts had been getting in the way of my happiness and that I had to get rid of them.

Quickly after that, a surprising thought crossed my mind. I actually felt as if there was a possibility that I could really get out of this bad situation and one day feel good about going to work.

I felt relieved and energized; I got moving and began to make things happen. I spoke to recruiters and soon found myself fielding offers.

*Within three months of starting to repeat my statement, I received a call from a colleague in my industry. He offered me a wonderful position with new challenges and responsibilities at a salary that was 30 percent **more** than what I was making!*

I've been with my new firm for quite a while. I love my job. Not only do I feel fulfilled, but it's terrific to finally be appreciated for what I do.

-S.L., Wayne, PA

Chapter 11

Willpower Loses Again

Most people, when they want to make a change in their lives, tend to do it the hard way. For example, if you are heavier than you want and you have decided to lose 20 pounds, you might choose to set a future date to begin a healthy eating and exercising plan. Then, on that date, you bravely wake up in the morning and boldly declare to yourself:

Today is the day I begin my diet!

A few hours later you may find yourself thinking about having a snack…and you quickly push that thought out of your mind.

Later on you may notice that other people in your office are snacking and again you think to yourself,

I wish I could have a donut, but I can't because I'm dieting.

Every once in a while you think about how nice it would be to eat something sweet and soft, and again, you try to push this thought away. The more you think about pushing the thought of eating sweets out of your mind, the more you seem to be thinking about sweets!

By the end of the day, you realize that you've been thinking about sweets all day. It's been a struggle to get through the day without snacking.

You managed to get through the day, but all day your thoughts have been about food and eating. You are not looking forward to the same old struggle with food tomorrow.

In this situation you are using every ounce of willpower to reach your goal of losing weight. It's been a huge struggle to try to change your eating habits and it's going to be a struggle tomorrow...and the next day...and the next day...and the next day.

It sure takes a lot of willpower to try to stay on track to lose weight, doesn't it?

Here's another example:

Imagine that I'm placing a 2 x 4 wooden board on the ground. Now I ask you to balance and walk carefully with one foot in front of the other down the length of the board. You look at the board and of course, you know it's easy to do, so you confidently walk from one end to the other.

Now I'm going to take that same 2 x 4 board and raise it 3 feet off the ground. Now when I ask you to walk the length of the board from one end to the other, your subconscious mind might shout, "NO!"

You were able to do it successfully when it was on the ground but now that it's 3 feet above the ground, it may seem scary to walk the length of the board.

Your subconscious mind is now quite nervous and wondering whether you'll be safe. Will you be able to walk steadily on the board and avoid falling?

You might feel that there is no way that you can now walk on that board. You'd have to use every ounce of willpower you can muster, but no amount of willpower is going to help you to stay safe. The only way you can be successful is if your subconscious stays confident and calm. If you can stay confident and calm, it's not a problem...just look at any gymnast on a balance beam.

YOUR SUBCONSCIOUS MIND ALWAYS WINS

Using your imagination (located in your subconscious mind) rather than your willpower (located in your conscious mind) is the secret to achieving your goal without struggling.

When you use your conscious mind, you want to be in control, but you probably won't believe that you can. When you use your imagination, it's easy to pretend or imagine how it will feel to choose to be in total control.

Since raising the wooden board three feet off the ground caused you to feel anxious and nervous, you now have a choice. You can choose to use your imagination to help you walk calmly across the plank of wood, or you can choose to try to walk while you are panicking and sweating.

In life you have many choices. You can choose to push through your fears with all the energy you can muster, or you can find a way to overcome them. You can choose to struggle, or you can choose to use Powerful Thinking on Purpose to help you reach your goals more easily. You are now learning how to take the struggle out of changes you desire in your life.

Your subconscious mind holds all of your emotions and given the choice between logic and emotion, emotions tend to win. Your imagination is the key to your happiness in life. Remember that your subconscious mind holds the most powerful part of you: your imagination.

For example, imagine that you are dieting. You have decided that you want to stay away from fats and sugars. You have been using your willpower all week and you've been sticking with your plan.

But now you find yourself at your local ice cream shop with your friends and they are all enjoying ice cream. "Come on, your friend encourages you, "just one scoop won't hurt you."

And now you find yourself thinking about smooth, cool, sweet ice cream…you can imagine the creamy sweetness on your tongue…and you are beginning to notice that your willpower is waning…you really do want to have some…but…you know you shouldn't…but you do really want it and one scoop won't make much of a difference….

You begin to notice that you are experiencing an internal struggle. Should you have a scoop? Your willpower finally runs out and you decide that one scoop is okay.

What part of you won that tiny battle?

Your conscious mind said, "I don't want to eat the ice cream," and then eventually (OK, rather quickly) ran out of willpower. Your subconscious mind, which holds all of your feelings, won that round because it knows how much you love ice cream.

Imagine Your Success

Think back to a time in your life when you achieved a goal and felt proud of yourself. Perhaps it was when you rode your bike without training wheels for the first time. Maybe it was the time you tried out for a team, started a business, or got hired after a successful interview. What were your thoughts before you began? What were your thoughts throughout the process? What were your thoughts afterwards?

Let's peek into the life of Matt, a culinary school graduate, who plans to open a new, unique, gourmet bakery. After his bakery becomes popular and achieves financial success, his goal is to turn the bakery into a national franchise. He has a flair for cake decorating and his chocolate chip cookies are legendary in his family. He's acquired the skills, knowledge, funding, and manpower to create a successful business.

SCENARIO 1:

Matt has been trying to be positive about opening his specialty bakery. But every time Matt imagines his bakery he sees himself standing behind the counter full of anxiety and worry.

He worries that not enough customers will return to create the repeat business he needs to be successful. He worries that he won't find enough good employees to work the demanding hours needed to run a flourishing bakery. Most of all, he worries that he might fail.

What kind of effect will these thoughts have on his goal? The more he thinks this way, the more he will eventually begin to believe that his bakery will never make it. He may even give up his longtime dream of his franchise.

Matt's thoughts will continue to repeat and drag him downward into a failing spiral. It's no surprise that his constant worries about personal failure will eventually affect his behavior. As a result of being bombarded with negative self-talk, Matt will give up. Eventually his willpower will get used up like a carton of milk, and he won't bother to take action. He won't be able to take the necessary first steps needed to achieve his dream of opening his bakery.

SCENARIO 2:

Matt understands how important his attitude is to his success. He realizes that he needs to change his self-talk and mindset to achieve his goal of owning a prosperous specialty bakery and franchise. He creates his powerful personal statement:

"I enjoy selling franchises of my bakery and I feel proud."

He uses his creative imagination to stay positive and imagine people calling him, excited about his franchise opportunity. He spends time thinking of creative ways to showcase his pastries. He researches and designs the layout of his bakery just the way he sees it in his mind. He takes time every day to imagine happy, satisfied customers lining up every morning to purchase coffee and delectable homemade cakes and pastries.

Every day he repeats his personal statement to reinforce his powerful imagination to see, feel, hear, smell, taste, and experience his perfect bakery.

Will he take the steps needed to open his bakery? Of course—nothing will get in his way when he is motivated!

Let's go back and look at SCENARIO 1. Matt's situation beautifully illustrates how easily willpower can run out. Willpower is like a gallon of milk; once it's used up, there's none left. It's easy to see why he would give up.

In SCENARIO 2, Matt uses his imagination to help him achieve his goal. Consequently, he remains positive and uses his powerful personal statement to keep himself on track and motivated.

Unlike his willpower, his imagination will never run out.

"Imagination is everything. It is the preview of life's coming attractions."

-ALBERT EINSTEIN

Chapter 12

Your Personal Protector

One of the functions of a healthy subconscious mind is to protect you. Your mind protects you from doing things that could cause you physical or emotional pain. You learned early on that touching fire will result in a painful burn. This knowledge is firmly and permanently implanted in your mind and prevents you from placing your hand on a hot stove.

Most likely, you've kept yourself safe and have never walked in the middle of a highway. You probably don't choose to put your life at risk by swimming in lagoons populated with hungry alligators either. You keep yourself safe and don't consciously put yourself in situations where you can get hurt.

Your subconscious mind also protects you from engaging in activities that might cause you to fail. For example, if you are aware that you are an average skier, you won't take the risk of hurting or embarrassing yourself by attempting to ski on the expert trails.

Your subconscious mind also protects you from creating personal inner conflicts. So if you believe that rich people are snobby and shallow, then you'll protect yourself from becoming rich, because you don't want to be considered snobby and shallow.

Young Minds

Our minds are very open when we are young. This is the time when we soak in everything around us. As babies and as children, we absorb information from the moment we are awake until the second we drift into sleep. We hear and learn from our parents, teachers, clergy, siblings, friends, TV, internet, movies, and radio.

It's no surprise that when we were young, we believed most of what we saw and heard. This is because young children don't have the same internal filters and judgment that adults have acquired. Therefore, children do not usually analyze what they notice around them. They don't ask themselves, "Is this something that is helpful for me to believe?" They don't intentionally choose to accept or reject a particular thought; they simply allow new thoughts to form, without question.

You might know that one of the most common fears among adults is the fear of public speaking. Some people even get so nervous and anxious when speaking in front of groups that they will do anything to get out of the situation.

Think of this scene. A mother and her seven-year-old daughter are getting ready to leave their house for the day. The mother is packing up her briefcase and she's talking to herself about how much she hates having to give the annual presentation at work. She's clearly nervous, and would prefer to avoid the situation.

Her daughter has been quietly playing and listening to her Mom's grumbling.

Can you imagine any seven year old saying this to her mother?

"Gee Mom, I understand that you have unresolved issues and complex anxieties about speaking in public, and while you choose to continue believing you can never speak comfortably in front of others, I have decided that this is your internal issue. I choose not to develop the same fear that you have."

Of course this would never happen. An adult might respond this way, but not a young child.

A more likely scenario is that the daughter remains silent while she listens to her mom. She might grow up thinking that it is normal to be anxious when speaking to groups. She may even have the belief that there is something frightening about speaking in public because she saw how nervous and upset her mom would get before a presentation.

Everything a child hears, notices, and experiences can pass directly into their subconscious mind, without question. As a result, we all tend to form opinions and beliefs based on our unfiltered experiences that can ultimately create limiting beliefs later in our lives.

Thankfully, with age and experience, your conscious mind has the maturity and the ability to question long-held beliefs.

As we get older, we don't automatically believe everything we are told. For example, if you meet your new next-door neighbor and she says "I'm Spiderman's mom," would you believe her? Of course not.

However, if this same neighbor tells your five-year-old-niece that she is Spiderman's mom, would your niece believe her?

Your niece might believe her without question because in her limited experience, all adults tell the truth. At the tender age of five, she hasn't created the filters in her mind that adults have learned to rely on. As young children, we tend to believe what we see and hear as truth even when it isn't.

For the record, the fictional character Mary Parker, who died in a plane crash with her husband Peter, was Spiderman's mom.

When we are children, we are rarely aware that our subconscious mind has been exposed to other people's worries and beliefs. When we are young, we often internalize others' beliefs and worries unwittingly. These internalized worries and beliefs can cause us personal struggles later in life. When this happens, we are at risk of experiencing life through other people's filters rather than our own.

Mark:

Mark is in 3rd grade and completing his math homework in the kitchen while his mom is cooking. He's quite engrossed in the process of memorizing his multiplication tables while his mother talks on the phone in the background.

Mom:

> *Thanks so much for inviting us to dinner on Saturday night, but my husband is away. I don't drive anywhere if I have to go over a bridge, and he won't be here to drive.*

While Mark's conscious mind is busy with homework, his subconscious mind is aware of everything going on around him. Mark has heard her say things like this before. He's never questioned it. He's never asked his friends if their moms have the same problem with driving over bridges. It's simply something he's overheard throughout his young life.

Remember that Mark doesn't have the tools and judgment that an adult has. He probably doesn't think or say to himself:

> *Wow. Mom certainly has an inconvenient fear. While I thoroughly understand that Mom has deep-seated issues about driving, this doesn't mean that I have to inherit her fear of driving over bridges.*

The reality is that when Mark hears his Mom repeatedly talking about her anxieties about driving, he probably accepts this as his truth too, without question. Internally, his subconscious may have decided something like this:

> *Gosh, I trust Mom. If Mom is scared of driving over bridges, there must be a good reason. I don't want to be scared or get hurt, so I'd better be really careful to avoid all bridges.*

From this moment forward Mark's subconscious mind will make sure that Mark doesn't cause himself undue harm by driving over a bridge. Just in case he doesn't remember how dangerous bridges are, his mind will protect him by creating a feeling of anxiety or panic when he thinks about or drives over a bridge.

Catherine:

Catherine is a bright, cheerful seven-year-old girl enjoying dinner with her family. After eating a serving of dessert, she reaches her hand out for an extra helping. At that very moment, she hears her mother remark to a guest at the dinner table:

I've struggled with weight all my life. It's been such a problem because the women in our family tend to be fat.

Catherine's mother is always talking about being fat and never being able to lose weight. As Catherine listens to her mother lament about weight, her subconscious mind interprets:

Because all the women in our family are fat, I guess I'm going to struggle with weight all my life and be fat too.

If Catherine was 18 and had heard her mother share this thought for the first time, she might purposely choose to think differently. She wouldn't accept this as truth because she would have the adult judgment to consciously reject her mother's belief.

She could choose to say this to herself:

I've noticed that all the women in our family are fat, but I can choose to be different.

Unfortunately, Catherine never got the chance to reject her mother's belief. Fast forward twenty years and we find that Catherine, just like all the women in her family, is now struggling with her weight.

Now she's decided to make a change. She wants to lose weight and become healthier. However, deep in her subconscious mind is this old belief:

...the women in our family always struggle with weight.

At a very early age, she absorbed this limiting belief about the women in her family. Do you think this might get in the way of her losing weight? I guarantee it will. The good news is that Catherine can change her thoughts and beliefs. And you can too.

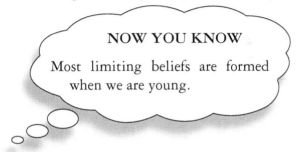

NOW YOU KNOW

Most limiting beliefs are formed when we are young.

Red Alert! Limiting Belief Forming Ahead!

One day I was driving with my eight-year-old son in the car. We were chatting about friends and relatives when he said:

"Mom, I never want to be rich."

"Why do you say that?" I responded.

"Well, rich people are crazy," he said.

"What do you mean?" I questioned.

"Mr. Smithson is kind of crazy and he has lots of money. I don't want to be crazy when I grow up so I don't want to be rich like him," he explained.

I was surprised to hear this. I had no idea why or how he put these two thoughts together. Our neighbor, Mr. Smithson has an unusual sense of humor, but crazy? No. Hmm... I thought... this sounds like a belief that might limit him later in his life. I'd better say something to help clear up his misconceptions about money causing people to be "crazy."

For the next few minutes, we talked about rich people and how all people are different regardless of the amount of money they make.

I asked him to think of a Disney Channel actor who he thought might make a lot of money selling CDs. After he named one, I asked him if he thought she was crazy.

"No," he replied, "I think she would be nice, just like the person she plays on TV."

The thought that "all rich people are crazy" was at the risk of becoming a belief. By simply helping him realize that people are different, regardless of the money they have, I helped him to avoid this limiting belief taking root in his subconscious mind.

Every time we help a person to clear up a misconception, we are helping them to stop limiting beliefs from *negatively affecting their lives.*

"The mind is a dutiful servant and will follow the instructions we give it."

-ZIG ZIGLAR

Chapter 13

Creating Effective Powerful Personal Statements

The key to Powerful Thinking on Purpose is to create powerful personal statements that will help you to feel better and be in control of your thoughts, beliefs, attitudes, actions, and habits.

In this chapter, you will learn how to form powerful personal statements that will *always work* for you. You'll be creating your own statements, custom designed by you, to propel yourself to success.

When you repeat your powerful personal statements every day, you can expect profound and measurable changes in how you feel and on your outlook on life.

Right now, the only things standing between you and your personal successes are your thoughts.

7 RULES FOR CREATING POWERFUL PERSONAL STATEMENTS

1. Your personal statement must be framed in the present.
2. Your personal statement must be positive.
3. Your personal statement must be simple.
4. Your personal statement must be believable.
5. Your personal statement must have a reward.
6. Your personal statement must feel true for you.
7. If it's not true for you, include the 5 Powerful Words: "I like the idea that..."

Keep reading and you'll learn how easy it is to create powerful personal statements that will change your life.

RULE 1: YOUR PERSONAL STATEMENT MUST BE FRAMED IN THE PRESENT TENSE.

Read the two sentences below:

1. I call two new prospects every day and I feel great.
2. I will call two new prospects every day and I will feel great.

Notice that there is a subtle difference between the two sentences.

Sentence A) is correctly stated in the present tense.

Sentence B) contains the word "will."

Remember, your subconscious mind is very literal. What you say is what you get. Also, your subconscious mind has no opinion, though it is your personal protector. So when you say to yourself:

I will call two new prospects every day and I will feel great.

your subconscious mind will hear the sentence EXACTLY as it is written. The definition of the word "will" is "going to." It means that what you are thinking of doing is going *to occur in the future* but hasn't happened yet.

So your subconscious will interpret this to mean:

At some time in the future, I don't really know when, it could be tomorrow, it could be next week, it could be next year, I'll call two new prospects every day and I will feel great.

If your goal is to start now, rather than sometime in the future, then it's imperative that you choose the correct words to describe your goal.

The preferred wording can be found in the statement below:

A) I call two new prospects every day and I feel great.

This statement works because it sounds like it's already part of your daily work routine. It happens today, tomorrow, and every day.

When forming your powerful personal statement, two words that are important to avoid are HOPE and TRY.

The word "hope" means to desire something with the expectation that it is likely to happen, but with the possibility that it might not. When you focus on hoping that something will happen, your subconscious frequently waffles back and forth between imagining that it will happen and imagining it won't happen.

Hoping causes conflicting thoughts in your subconscious mind.

The definition of "try" is: To make an attempt or effort.

Because your subconscious mind takes words literally, this means that if you "try" something, you are attempting something, *not actually doing* it. If you decide to *try* to bake a loaf of bread today what you are really saying is that you are going to attempt to bake a loaf of bread.

Will you really bake a loaf of bread today? Maybe you will or maybe you won't. But you might try.

When you say you will *"try,"* you are NOT stating that you will accomplish your task.

> *"Try not.*
> *Do, or do not.*
> *There is no try."*
>
> -Yoda

Years ago, when my daughter was younger, I would remind her to clean her room.

She said, "I'll try to do it, Mom." And she did. Sometimes she organized her room, but often she didn't. When she was a teenager and understood what the word "try" meant, she often responded with "I'm doing my best!" She quickly learned the power of language.

TIP: Keep the words *will, hope,* and *try* out of your powerful personal statements.

RULE 2: YOUR PERSONAL STATEMENT MUST BE POSITIVE.

Your subconscious mind often ignores negative words, so it's more effective to focus on what you want. Anytime your subconscious hears a negative word such as *"don't"* or *"won't,"* these words are as *good as ignored.*

TAKE A MOMENT FOR YOURSELF NOW:

Imagine that I am saying the following three sentences to you. Read all three of them first and then do them as an exercise:

1. Close your eyes.
2. Take a deep breath.
3. DON'T imagine a pink elephant in your mind.

What just happened? Most likely, 75 percent of you briefly saw a pink elephant in your mind. The other 25 percent imagined a pink elephant for a brief moment and then quickly tried to erase it or turn your mind blank.

Either way, the image of a pink elephant appeared—even for a split second.

This occurred because your subconscious mind MUST imagine the pink elephant before you can delete it.

Essentially your subconscious ignored the word "DON'T" and interpreted the third sentence as

Imagine a pink elephant in your mind.

This wasn't exactly what you intended. You wanted to make sure that you DID NOT imagine a pink elephant!

When someone who wants to lose weight continually says the sentence below, what are they really saying?

I don't want to crave chocolate.

The subconscious eliminates the word *"don't"* and interprets the thought like this:

I want to crave chocolate.

This is what your subconscious mind hears and processes. Is this what you intended? Of course not. No wonder things don't always work out the way you want!

How you talk to yourself is essential to your personal success or failure. The words you choose are extremely important in achieving your goal.

Read the two sentences below. Which one do you think will work best to help you reach your goal?

A: *I don't want to overeat at dinner.*

B: *I choose to eat small portions at dinner.*

If you answered B) then you now understand the power of self-talk and the power of your words.

To put it simply,

> **When you think about what you want,
> you get what you want.**
>
> **When you think about what you don't want,
> you get what you don't want.**

TIP: Keep your personal statements positive. Eliminate *"don't,"* *"won't,"* and other negative words.

NOW YOU KNOW

When you say a sentence to yourself that includes the word "don't," your subconscious mind often cannot process or recognize it. It's as if the word is deleted from the sentence.

RULE 3: YOUR PERSONAL STATEMENT MUST BE SIMPLE.

Because you'll be repeating your powerful statement throughout the day, it's important to make sure that it's simple. It's much easier to remember a simple sentence than a complex one. Read the two sets of examples below and decide which of the following sentences would be easier to repeat ten times daily.

EXAMPLE A:

Every time I eat, I make sure that I consume just the right amount of healthy fresh fruits and crunchy fresh vegetables that provide me with all the beneficial nutrients and vitamins I require, and are easily absorbed into my body so that I feel energetic all day.

EXAMPLE B:

I eat five fruits and veggies every day and I feel great.

and

EXAMPLE A:

Every day I do everything I can to research and learn what industries and careers are best suited to my personality, so that I can start and manage my own business, work for myself, hire my own employees, and create a successful career that is meaningful and fulfilling.

EXAMPLE B:

I am my own boss and I love what I do.

In each of the above examples, it's easier to remember the second sentence. When your personal statement is easy to remember, you'll find it easier to repeat.

Some people find it fun to create personal statements that rhyme. Feel free to do this as long as it remains simple. For example, if you wanted to exercise more, you might say, "Every time I run, I have a lot of fun."

Remember: Keep your powerful personal statements simple.

SUCCESS STORY

When I was single a few years back, I used to wake up and say with power and feeling "I am happily married to a wonderful, successful man." And 3 years later I am! I met him 3-6 months after repeating my powerful personal statement on a regular basis. When I was making $10 an hour at a job that was making me miserable, I used to drive to work and yell and scream at the top of my lungs with power and intensity—"I make 60K a year in a job I love!" Within 6 months of doing this on an almost daily basis, I found a job I loved and made that much within the first year. The next year I made 80K.

-Jasmine Kaloudis, Synergy by Jasmine, Yoga Instructor, Philadelphia, PA

RULE 4: YOUR PERSONAL STATEMENT MUST BE BELIEVABLE.

Simply put, this means that your personal statement must be something that you believe you can accomplish.

If you want to become the next big rock star and you don't know how to play the guitar, then most likely you have a long way to go before the end result will be believable. However, it can be believable when you chunk your goal into smaller ones. For example, "I take guitar lessons once a week."

It's important to set up outcomes for yourself that are believable. When we set up goals for ourselves that are too overwhelming, we tend to do one of two things: We either freeze up and don't even bother to begin, or we start and then quickly give up because we feel we'll never be able to reach our goal.

How many times you have made a New Year's resolution? How many of your resolutions lasted throughout the year?

It's no surprise that the first quarter of the year is the most popular time for health clubs to gain new members. The fact is that 50 percent of all new health club members quit within the first six months of signing up. Most people join with the intention of exercising frequently. ("I'm going to exercise five days a week now that I've joined the gym.") They set their expectations so high that when they miss a few days, they feel that they have failed. They have completely overwhelmed themselves with their commitment. Rather than start slowly and achieve small successes, they give up because their goal was too difficult.

When most people think about losing a lot of weight, the thought of shedding so many pounds feels almost impossible. Rather than thinking about losing such a large amount of weight, you'll have much more success when you break your weight goal into smaller, achievable steps. This concept tends to be true for most large goals.

Just like adding exercise into a daily routine, when people choose to lose weight, they tend to focus on their big goal. "I want to lose sixty pounds."

For some people, the thought of losing sixty pounds is overwhelming. They begin to feel frustrated when they think about how many days and how many months it will take to achieve their goal. Most people begin with the intention of sticking with their goal, but saddled with the overwhelming prospect, will ultimately give up.

Remember that when you break your goal down into smaller pieces, it will be easier to achieve. It's easier to believe that small successes are possible. Doesn't losing three or five pounds feel more achievable than sixty pounds? Sure it does. And after you've successfully lost five pounds, it will be easy to lose the next five pounds, and the next. Losing weight can be easier and a lot more manageable when you keep your goals small.

After you have decided to take a smaller step, then you'll need to make a new decision. What will you do differently to lose the first three to five pounds? Take your time to decide how you are going to achieve your goal of losing weight in smaller chunks.

You already know that the best way to lose weight is to change what you are doing. You know you need to change your eating habits and exercise more. If one of your bad habits is eating too many sweets, perhaps you decide that from this day forward you will no longer eat anything that contains sugar in any form. Nothing. Ever. You know that sugar is bad for you. It puts fat on your body. It is nutritionally useless. You are completely and forever finished with sugar.

Here is the statement that you begin with:

From now on I choose to keep away from any food that contains sugar and I feel great.

Read it again and ask yourself the following questions:

Is this believable?

Will I miss eating foods with sugar?

Will I feel deprived if I never taste ice cream for the rest of my life?

Think about your answers. Be honest with yourself. If sugar has been part of your diet, and you like it, then it's logical to think that you will have a difficult time avoiding sweets.

What will happen the first time you eat a piece of chocolate? Will you feel guilty? Will you feel bad that you failed and couldn't keep away from sugar?

Generally, feeling guilt or regret can result in needless eating, especially if you are an emotional eater. You really don't want to go there.

You can, however, consider an alternate way of eating. One that reduces the amount of sugar consumption, allows you to enjoy something you love, and avoids negative feelings.

Some people have an addiction to sugar, and for those people, it might be necessary to quit eating sweets forever. Ask yourself which of the following is believable. Which one feels better to you?

A) *From now on, I choose to no longer eat foods that contain sugar and I feel great.*

B) *Every day I allow myself to eat 50 calories of sweets and I feel proud.*

In my opinion, there is no right or wrong way to lose weight as long as you do it in a healthy way. Whichever statement you choose must feel right for you, though. If you repeat the statement in your mind and it's not believable, you'll know it. Some people tend to choose what they feel they "should" be doing. If you notice that you have a "should" feeling inside of you, then it's a good idea to change your statement because you might be setting yourself up for failure. If this is something that you "want" to do, it will be much easier to follow through and stay motivated. If you are doing something because you feel you "should," then you might have a tough time and find yourself struggling to achieve your goal.

RULE 5: YOUR PERSONAL STATEMENT MUST HAVE A REWARD.

I'm not talking about a reward such as a wad of cash or a new car. What I mean by a reward is that there must be something positive and good that you will achieve as a result of reaching your objectives and goals.

It's human nature to either want to do things that avoid pain or take action that results in feeling good. For example, when we go to work, we get a reward in the form of a paycheck. A paycheck is a good incentive to get up in the morning and go to work. It goes without saying that most people would choose to stay home if they didn't receive their reward of money.

Another example of a reward is the one that happens when you lose weight. The main reasons for losing weight are to look good, feel great, and enjoy improved health. These are wonderful rewards! Would you bother losing weight if you knew that you would not look and feel good? Would you bother losing weight if your health didn't improve?

Here are some examples of rewards that you can put at the end of your personal statement:

- I feel great.
- I am satisfied.
- I am proud of myself.

Many people who want to get over their anxieties about speaking in public are willing to do whatever it takes to overcome this common fear. When their fear is gone, the benefits and rewards can be plentiful. An entrepreneur can easily present his proposal to investors, an aspiring actor can overcome audition jitters, and a vice president can calmly share new concepts with his team.

The rewards for getting over the fear of speaking might be:

- I am calm.
- I am relaxed.
- I have more success.

Feeling good is the best motivator on the planet.

RULE 6: YOUR PERSONAL STATEMENT MUST FEEL TRUE FOR YOU.

This is by far the most important rule. If this rule is ignored, then repeating your personal statement is simply a waste of time. If your statement doesn't feel true for you, then it's no more effective than a generic affirmation you might read in a book.

Every personal statement you create must be tested in your mind to determine how it feels for you. This crucial step is necessary so that your subconscious mind will accept your statement and you can achieve success.

This is your turning point. Ignore this rule and you'll never move forward. You'll continually be blocked by your subconscious mind that wants to protect you. When you follow this rule it will lead to great success.

One of my clients, I'll call him Dave, had the goal of being a relaxed and comfortable speaker when he addressed large groups of people. Consciously he knew this was possible. He knew many others who were calm when speaking to a group. When he was in fourth grade, he was totally comfortable presenting his book report to his class. In fact, he had fun playing the parts of the major characters as he told the story to his peers.

Years later, during his junior year of high school, Dave had a life changing experience. In his history class, he stood up to answer a question and his mind went completely blank. One of his friends knew that Dave was smart and could answer almost any history question that was thrown at him. But when he saw the blank look on Dave's face, he couldn't help himself and laughed out loud.

Fast forward to today and now whenever Dave speaks to a group of people, he begins to sweat, his heart pounds, and his mind goes blank for the first few moments. He's able to finish his speech, but it's always quite painful for him. He's experiencing a true fear: the very common fear of speaking in public.

Even though his conscious mind knows that he will be safe when he speaks, his subconscious mind is screaming in fear, worried that something bad will happen or that people will laugh and make fun of him.

To try to overcome his discomfort, Dave creates the following personal statement for himself:

I am comfortable whenever I speak in front of a group.

As he repeats his statement, he hears a little voice inside say:

Who are you kidding? You know you will panic and people will laugh at you.

You have learned that your subconscious mind always wants to protect you. Its primary goal is to keep you safe. It's clear that Dave's subconscious mind does not believe he will be safe when he speaks in front of a group.

Dave then creates a new positive statement to help himself when he speaks in public:

> *I like the idea that I am comfortable whenever I speak in front of a group.*

As Dave repeats his new personal statement, he notices that he's smiling. He really does like this idea.

Dave continued to repeat his personal statement for the next few weeks. The morning of his team presentation at work, he was pleased to find that he actually felt peaceful and relaxed. He calmly delivered his presentation and when he finished, he sat down and smiled to himself. He was thrilled that he finally felt comfortable giving a presentation at work. Soon after, he decided to join Toastmasters International to improve his presentation skills. Dave is quite the success story and now is actively involved in Toastmasters, helping others improve their speaking skills.

EXAMPLE 1: Meredith's Powerful Personal Statement

Meredith was a divorced woman who wanted to lose about twenty pounds. After leaving a very difficult marriage, she realized it was time to feel good about herself and get back into the world of dating. She was tired of yo-yo dieting, tired of everything related to dieting. From her extensive readings she learned that she simply needed to focus her energy on changing her lifestyle. She added exercise into her daily routine, and shifted her eating patterns.

She said her personal statement frequently:

I am at my perfect weight of 130 pounds and I am healthy and happy.

She was doing really well and in three quick months she had lost fifteen pounds. But something changed. For the next four months, she didn't lose a pound. She struggled and struggled to lose weight. She would lose a pound, and then gain a pound. She became frustrated and angry with herself. She felt thoroughly stuck.

Meredith knew that something was getting in her way of losing weight and achieving success, but she had no idea what it was, nor did she have any idea what to do about it.

She confided her feelings about being stuck to her close friend. Her friend thoughtfully asked her what had happened the last time she weighed less.

When Meredith was ten years old, her father had an affair and her parents went through a nasty divorce. She remembered overhearing her mother in another room yelling, "I trusted you! I never should have trusted my judgment in you!" Young Meredith felt sad for her mother and angry at her father. She knew she wasn't supposed to eavesdrop, so she wasn't able to share her feelings with her parents. Consequently she ate and ate to numb her feelings and by the time she was 21, she tipped the scale at over 180 pounds.

By age 24, she began to feel better about herself and started to work out and make healthy food choices. Slowly but surely, by the time she reached 26, she was down to 130 pounds. She began to date and got married two years later. Within a year of her wedding, her weight began to creep up.

Meredith remembered feeling as if she was a failure early in the marriage. She had trusted her judgment and had married a man she thought was perfect for her. This was far from the truth. She caught her husband having an affair, and after ten years in an unfulfilled and unhappy marriage, she divorced him.

As she was relating her story to her friend, Meredith realized that there was a connection between being thinner and trusting her judgment in men. She realized at that moment that if she lost weight and looked great, that there would be no more excuses for staying home on Saturday nights.

If she lost weight, she would be attractive to men and might be asked to go out on a date. In that brief moment, she knew that if she went out on a date, she might end up getting serious with a man. She knew that she couldn't trust her judgment about men because her judgment had failed her in the past. In the end, she felt she would be sad and hurt.

That evening when she said her personal statement,

I am at my perfect weight of 130 pounds and I am healthy and happy,

she felt a disconnect. She heard a little voice in the back of her mind whisper:

yeah, but...

Something didn't feel right. While her statement was in the present tense and was positive, simple, and believable, it just didn't feel true for her. She was holding onto two limiting beliefs.

One was:

My judgment about men is always wrong.

The other was:

When I'm thinner, I might get into a relationship with a man who doesn't make me happy.

She knew she had to do some work in order to let go of her old limiting beliefs.

Meredith made the decision that while she was going to examine ways to eliminate her old beliefs, she would also pay attention to her weight.

She created a new personal statement in that moment by adding the 5 Powerful Words:

*I **like the idea that** I weigh 130 pounds and I am happy and healthy.*

She said it out loud and did a quick internal check to notice if she had any resistance. None showed up. She knew that her new powerful personal statement would work for her because it felt 100 percent true.

EXAMPLE 2: Michael's Powerful Personal Statement

Michael decided to leave his full time job to become a software consultant specializing in helping small businesses identify productivity solutions based on their specific goals. He is a knowledgeable and confident professional as a result of his 25 years of experience in the field.

He has successfully created a business plan, priced his services competitively, and completed his legal documents. His potential prospect list already includes some friends who own small businesses and who have been looking forward to Michael's help.

Michael knows that it's easy for him to get sidetracked during the workday, but he knows that to have a successful business, he must sign up quality clients. His goal is to sign up five clients within the next few months. He decides to call on one new prospect each day.

His personal statement is:

It's easy for me to sign up great clients and I am excited about my business.

As Michael reads his statement again, he closes his eyes and sees an image of himself in his new office. He's on the phone with a client who is thanking him and mentioning other ways in which they need his help. He's smiling and happy.

Michael can tell that this statement feels true for him and begins to repeat it that evening. The next day he's smiling and happily calling his first prospect. He is feeling excited about his new business.

DID YOU KNOW?

If you are thinking about doing something that is in conflict with your inner beliefs, your subconscious mind will step in to try to keep you from getting hurt.

EXAMPLE 3: Stephen's Powerful Personal Statement

Stephen recently graduated from college with a degree in finance. He is looking for a job that pays well, and where he can enjoy helping others achieve their financial goals. He creates this personal statement:

I work at a great job where I help a lot of people and make a lot of money.

He sits down, closes his eyes, and repeats his positive statement five times. But his statement just doesn't ring true. It doesn't seem to fit well, like a bulldog being pushed into a mouse hole. He notices an odd feeling, as if he is trying to fool himself into believing something that isn't true.

While he is thinking, a hazy image begins to form and he sees himself as a young boy overhearing his father complain about his job:

"I can't believe I went to college and I can barely make enough to support our family."

He remembers that his father would grumble and complain every month when he opened the envelope containing his meager paycheck.

Stephen recognizes that these are his father's words, thoughts, and beliefs. He also clearly realizes that what happened to his father doesn't have to happen in his life. Stephen can choose a different path and enjoy a successful career. He doesn't have to share his father's belief.

Stephen's personal statement was stated in the present and was positive, simple, and believable, but it just didn't feel true for him. He knew he had to let go of this limiting belief that took root when he was a child.

He decided to create a new personal statement by adding the 5 Powerful Words. His new personal statement works for him because it is now 100 percent true.

Stephen's new statement is:

> *I like the idea that* I have a great job where I help people and make lots of money.

Anytime you say a personal statement and it doesn't feel true for you, you have smacked into your own personal barrier. This barrier indicates that there is something inside you—most likely an erroneous thought, or a limiting belief—that will block you from achieving your success.

Remember, it's not intended to block you from your goal, rather it is your subconscious mind doing its job to PROTECT you.

RULE 7: IF IT'S NOT TRUE FOR YOU, INCLUDE THE 5 POWERFUL WORDS.

It's human nature to want to postpone tasks that don't offer an obvious reward for completion. A good example is doing taxes. Many people put their taxes off until the last moment. They don't feel a great incentive to sit down, fill out paperwork, and then write a check.

Until last year, I always put my taxes off until the last few weeks. Even though I thought I was ignoring my taxes, in reality I was causing myself undue stress because I was still thinking about my taxes every day. "I have to do my taxes today" was a thought that went through my mind a couple of times each day from January through March.

This year I decided to reduce my stress and changed how I thought about doing my taxes by repeating this statement daily:

I easily and quickly complete my taxes and I feel great!

I looked at my personal statement and read it out loud. Of course I liked the idea of completing something and feeling great.

I read it a second time and noticed that something didn't feel quite right. I noticed that this statement made me feel like I was trying to force myself into believing something that wasn't true. The word "quickly" bothered me; it didn't feel possible. Besides, I don't really love paying my taxes, but I do feel grateful for the benefits we get in the USA that are funded by our taxes.

The first thing I did was to take out the word "quickly":

I easily complete my taxes before April and I feel great.

There was still something about my statement that didn't feel 100 percent true. It felt about 60 percent true. I had no clue why it wasn't true, but I knew I had hit a wall of resistance.

I knew that if it wasn't true, I wouldn't achieve my stated goal. It was time to change my statement and preface it with the 5 Powerful Words:

I like the idea that

Here was my new statement:

I like the idea that I easily complete my taxes before April and I feel great!

I read it again. Of course I like this idea. Once I mail my taxes, I know that I won't be thinking about them for at least another ten months. Getting them done and out of the way will definitely free my mind from the subject and reduce my stress.

Adding the 5 Powerful Words shifted my personal statement from just 60 percent to <u>100 percent believable.</u>

After repeating my powerful personal statement for a week, I became aware that I couldn't wait to finish my taxes and get them out of the way. This was definitely a new experience for me. For the first time, I finished and mailed them before February 1st. I felt great about it too!

I Like The Idea That...

These 5 Powerful Words have the power to propel a positive statement instantly from 60 percent believable to 100 percent believable. They even have the ability to take your statement from 10 percent to 100 percent. Your 5 Powerful Words have the power to *increase the strength* of your personal statement quickly and effortlessly. You can think of it as a magic accelerant for your personal success.

One benefit of adding these 5 Powerful Words is that once your subconscious mind accepts your personal statement as true for you, things may rapidly begin to change.

Many people notice that at some point they naturally stop using the 5 Powerful Words. They become aware that they are now repeating their earlier, shorter statement. When this happens to you, see it as your personal indicator that you have successfully internalized your powerful personal statement and now believe this to be true for you.

Now that your personal statement is TRUE FOR YOU, your subconscious mind will *accept it as truth and allow you to reach your goal without being held back by old limiting beliefs.*

Chapter 14

See, Feel, Hear, Repeat

After you have created your powerful personal statement, you need to add a few simple ingredients to the mix to make it work faster and easier. This is really the fun part of Powerful Thinking on Purpose. Not only will you feel great in the moment, you get to focus your thoughts on what you want, which ultimately helps you reach your desired goal. You'll be doing this daily by using your powerful imagination.

What we think about, we attract to ourselves. Remember the concept of plants, flowers, and bushes in your garden attracting birds, butterflies, and insects? Your thoughts also attract things, feelings, and the ability to see opportunities.

When you think negative thoughts, what happens? You start to feel bad, frustrated, unhappy, angry, or sad.

When you think positive thoughts, what happens? You start to feel calm, relaxed, empowered, and excited.

Below are four important steps to help you feel and experience what it will be like to achieve success. In the process you'll also get the bonus of feeling good.

SEE

The Widescreen TV Technique

Imagine that right in front of you is a large flat screen TV. A picture of you having *already* achieved your goal is right there on the screen in full, bright color. You might imagine yourself in a beautiful new office. You could see yourself on the vacation of a lifetime with your family. Maybe see yourself balancing your accounts and all of them holding large amounts of money. Perhaps you imagine that you are walking and holding hands with your perfect partner. Have fun with your imagination here. There are no limits!

Next, in your mind, enlarge your TV until it is life-size.

Now, imagine that you can step right into that image of you. It's as easy as putting on a costume. You put your feet in first, then your arms, and then your head. You pull up the zipper and *voila!* You now ARE the new you! Notice how it feels now that you are in your new body of success. Feel it. Experience it. Look around you. What do you see? How do you look? Imagine how great you look after having reached your goal and knowing that you can achieve anything you want.

NOTE: At this point, it's OK to pretend that you are in your new body. You don't have to imagine it in full detail or color. Simply pretend that it's happening.

HEAR

Now as you imagine yourself as this new, successful "you" in your TV, you must say your powerful personal statement. Repeat it ten times while you are the new you in the TV. You can say it in your mind or out loud. Either way, you'll experience the same result. While you are saying your statement, feel what it feels like to be this new you. Hear yourself repeating your personal statement while you are in your new body of success.

FEEL

You can now maximize the power of your personal statement by adding positive feelings while you are imagining yourself in your success picture. While you are repeating your statement, you can pretend or *imagine* that you have reached your goal. *Feel* how great it *feels* to be successful, slim, happy, etc. Keep on feeling these feelings and notice how great you feel inside.

Your success picture can be still or moving. How you imagine it is up to you. Some people like to see themselves doing something they enjoy, either by themselves or with friends and family. When you allow your creative mind to come up with fun and positive scenes, you'll find it's easy to want to put yourself in them even more often.

One fun way is to imagine yourself calling a friend and sharing how great you are feeling now that you have achieved your goal:

Guess what? I did it! I feel great!

You can add even more by hearing your friend respond. Notice how good you feel when your friend says:

Wow. You are awesome. You did it. I'm proud of you!

Have fun with this scene. Make it feel even more amazing. Take this image in your mind and grow it until it becomes life-size. Imagine yourself in your favorite colors. Look at that smile on your face. You feel great. You look great. Notice all the sounds, sights, and feelings of this awesome scene.

REPEAT

Changing your subconscious thoughts using the techniques you've learned in this book is a great way for you to reduce your stress and achieve your goals. If you come across a personal issue that seems to have many limiting beliefs and you are feeling overwhelmed, then you might want to consider seeing a professional, such as a coach or certified hypnotist.

Repeating your powerful personal statement helps you to feel better every day. Every time you repeat it, you will be creating feelings of optimism, hopefulness, anticipation, enthusiasm, and happiness. In the moment when you focus on something that you want, you send a wonderful positive feeling throughout your mind and body.

Remember when you learned how to drive a car? For the first five, ten, or twenty times you drove, you had to take time to recall where the horn, radio, windshield wipers, heater, and brakes were located. After a few weeks, when you got in the car, you automatically knew where everything was located. Driving became second nature.

The more you intentionally create powerful thoughts on purpose, the more you will automatically access them subconsciously. The more you focus on your powerful personal statements, the more positive thoughts you'll be creating. Imagine how much better you'll feel when positive thoughts become second nature to you.

TIP: For additional reinforcement, you might want to write your personal statement on a piece of paper several times a day. Every time you write, you can intentionally put yourself in the place that feels good—as if you have already achieved success. The more you feel, hear, and see yourself as successful, the more this thought will become integrated in your subconscious mind.

Say your powerful personal statements every day. Frequent practice is much more effective than sporadic practice. When you practice them consistently, you create a powerful compounding effect that helps your subconscious accept your positive statement much more quickly.

The best way to start your day is to repeat your personal statement ten times in the morning—before you put your feet on the floor. Then repeat it again 10 times right before you go to sleep. Another great time to repeat them is when you exercise or walk. Anytime you are doing something that doesn't require concentration, you can repeat your personal statement.

You can't overdo reinforcement.

Remember: See, Feel, Hear, Repeat

Chapter 15

You Didn't Learn This in School

Every day you have thousands and thousands of thoughts. If you were to write every thought you had on a piece of paper, you might notice that most of them are repetitive old thoughts. Most likely, many of them are worries, fears, and general negative thoughts. Your awareness of your thoughts is the first step toward making a positive change that will help you feel good and open the doors to new possibilities.

According to Brian Wansink, *Mindless Eating – Why We Eat More Than We Think*, New York: Bantam-Dell, 2006, we make over 200 decisions about food each day. Add this to the other decisions we make, for example, what to wear, where to go, what to read, what to tackle first at work, what sites to visit on the web, where to drive, etc., and it's easy to realize that we do indeed have thousands of thoughts daily.

When you notice that you are thinking about something that you don't want, you can quickly change that thought to feel better and be in control of your actions. Remember that your thoughts affect your beliefs. Your beliefs directly affect your attitude, and your attitude directly affects your actions.

An easy way to determine if you are thinking about things you don't want is below:

**When you feel bad,
you are thinking about something that *you don't want.*
When you feel good,
you are thinking about something that *you do want.***

Remember from Chapter 8, Staying Calm in an Uncertain World, that whenever you are worrying about something you cannot control, you can stop for a moment and think about a positive outcome. You can imagine what you want. Then add your 5 Powerful Words in front of your thought.

You Always Have a Choice

When I was growing up, our family went to visit my grandparents for a family dinner most weekends. I remember my father saying to me, "You always have a choice, Wen. You can go to your grandparents' house and choose to be miserable, or you can go to your grandparents' house and choose to have a good time."

Even at age seven, I knew this was a no-brainer. I made the choice to enjoy myself while visiting my grandparents. It was that easy.

When I was a teenager, I felt as if I had very few choices in my life. I couldn't choose to do what I wanted, when I wanted. My parents put limits on me that were not my choice. *("What do you mean I have to be home by midnight?")* As a young adult, I felt that society was limiting me too. As I got older, I felt as if I had fewer and fewer choices.

Many years later, David Crump, a brilliant man who created the Essential Experience Workshop, made a profound statement that changed my life. I was in the perfect place in my personal development to hear and incorporate his insight into all aspects of my life. Simply and clearly, he said,

> *You can choose your thoughts.*

His suggestion changed my life. I want it to change yours too.

The Power of Thought Can Save a Life

One of the worst situations a person can experience is to be a prisoner of war.

I'm sure you have read or heard many horror stories of life as a prisoner of war in WWII. While millions of Jews died in the horrific conditions of the concentration camps, there were also some who survived. What was true for everyone at every moment in their terrible experience was that each person had a choice—they could still choose their thoughts.

Viktor Frankl was a man who survived three Nazi death camps because he learned that he had the freedom to choose his thoughts, regardless of how horrendous the situation was for him. In his bestselling book, *Man's Search For Meaning*, he wrote:

> *"Everything can be taken from a man, but...the last of the human freedoms—to choose one's attitude in any given set of circumstances, to choose one's own way."*
>
> -VIKTOR FRANKL

No matter what the situation is, we have the free will and ability to intentionally choose our thoughts. In any given situation there can be more than one outcome. For example, when someone goes to a job interview, he might get the job, or he might not. The hurricane that is heading towards a city might come in with full force, or fizzle to a light rain.

Viktor Frankl found the escape he needed from the desolation of his daily life. He chose to contemplate the image he carried of his beloved wife and to focus on his spirituality. The Nazis could destroy many things, but were unable to destroy his thoughts. Viktor Frankl used his mind to help him adapt and ultimately become a survivor.

Not only can your thoughts help you to feel better in the moment, your thoughts may be the difference between death and life.

YOU HAVE LEARNED WHAT YOU DIDN'T LEARN IN SCHOOL

Throughout this book you have learned that what stops you from moving forward in life are fears attached to limiting beliefs. Those fears are simply negative thoughts about something in the future that hasn't happened.

The opposite of that negative thought is the thought of your desired outcome. You've learned how to create powerful personal statements that allow you to focus on your desired outcome in a way that is believable. This believability is necessary for your subconscious mind to accept the outcome you have intentionally chosen. You'll find that it's much easier to achieve success when your subconscious believes in what you want, rather than when you are pushing yourself to achieve your goals.

Most important is that you've learned the benefits of intentionally changing your thoughts. When you are facing situations over which you have no control, you can easily use your powerful personal statements to reduce your stress. Reducing stress and feeling good in the moment are added benefits to powerful thinking.

Choosing to take control of your thoughts is something you can do anytime you want. No one can take this away from you. The more you control your thoughts, the better you'll feel.

My wish for you is that you take what you have learned in Powerful Thinking on Purpose, use it daily, share it with your friends, relatives, and even your children. The concepts you have learned in this book are not taught in school and every person can benefit from them tremendously, regardless of age.

To help you get started today, I've created easy-to-use worksheets that you'll find at the end of this book. These worksheets can help you motivate yourself. This is a great time to think of those things that you may have been putting off for a long time. You'll be accomplishing your goal much more easily because you will be using your powerful personal statement. Use these worksheets right now and put your new knowledge to use.

The good news is that you have already begun to incorporate these new concepts at your subconscious level just by reading this book.

Just imagine the amazing directions your life can take when you use Powerful Thinking on Purpose....

NOW YOU KNOW

Make sure your thoughts always reflect your desires because your life will always go in the direction of your thoughts.

SHARE YOUR SUCCES STORIES!

Have other people's success stories motivated and inspired you? Won't you share your story and inspire others? I'm compiling success stories from readers who create powerful personal statements and achieve personal and/or professional success.

When people read your story and learn how easy it is to change their thoughts and achieve success, they'll be inspired to do this for themselves.

Please email your personal success stories (no matter how big or how small) to:

wendy@PowerfulThinkingOnPurpose.com

I know you will accomplish wonderful things with

Powerful Thinking on Purpose.

"You can choose to think wonderful thoughts that make you feel good, or you can choose to think thoughts that make you feel miserable. It is always your choice."

-WENDY MERRON

RESOURCES

I invite you to visit our websites. You'll find community, support, tips, workshops, and programs that will help you to incorporate Powerful Thinking on Purpose into your daily life. It's fun to hang out with positive people.

http://www.PowerfulThinkingOnPurpose.com/Success:
This page is for you. Commit to your success. Sign up for my weekly Powerful Tips. Check out helpful and inspirational articles to help you stay positive and enjoy life more!

https://hypnotherapytrainer.com/home
Learn Hypnosis for yourself or get Certified as a Hypnotist to help others. Join like-minded friends in my interactive and fun 10 Week Online Training Class.

http://www.TheCenterOfSuccess.com:
For those of you in the Philadelphia area. Please check out our Workshops, Training, and Personal Sessions in Wayne, PA

Join SHARING POSITIVITY: Our Google+ Community
Learn tips to be more positive, post personal success, read and share positive quotes, support and inspire others.
http://tinyurl.com/d2hbbev

Appendix

Powerful Thinking on Purpose™ Worksheets

Rules for Powerful Personal Statements:

1. Your statement must <u>be in the present tense.</u>
2. Your statement must <u>be positive.</u>
3. Your statement must <u>be simple.</u>
4. Your statement must <u>be believable.</u>
5. Your statement must <u>have a reward.</u>
6. Your statement must <u>feel true for you.</u>
7. If it's not true for you, include the 5 Powerful Words: <u>I like the idea that…</u>

SAMPLE POWERFUL PERSONAL STATEMENT IDEAS

Below are some helpful and powerful words that you can use to create your personal statements. Of course you can make up your own too. These are phrases just to get you started. Remember to add the 5 Powerful Words in front of your personal statement if you need them. You can mix and match the ones from each column.

Use these at the beginning	Use these words at the end
I like the idea that	and I have more energy
Every day I	and I feel great
I allow myself	and I am calm and relaxed
I choose to	and I am proud of myself
It's easy for me	and I feel satisfied
Every time I	and I feel wonderful
I take time to	and I feel empowered

Personal Statement Examples:

Every day I walk for 10 minutes and I feel wonderful.

It's easy for me to give presentations and I am proud of myself.

Every time I drive on the highway, I am calm and relaxed.

I like the idea that I am focused at work and I feel great.

Personal Goal Worksheets

Take a moment to think of some personal goals you want to achieve. These can be small goals, such as organizing your workspace, or larger goals, for example, getting a college degree.

Depending on what your goals are, some may have only one step, while others may have three or more tasks associated with them.

During the process of completing what you need to do, you might find that some steps get delayed while you wait for information or responses from others. You may find that you need to add more steps that you hadn't thought of when you first began the process.

You might want to consider working on three goals at a time. Make your first ones fairly easy so you can show yourself how easy and simple it is to use Powerful Thinking on Purpose to achieve your desires.

EXAMPLE

THREE GOALS I WANT TO ACHIEVE:

1. *Get over fear about speaking in public*

2. *Organize office*

3. *Learn Italian*

Write Goal #1 below. Think of ways you can break it down into small action steps and write them below too:

GOAL # 1: Get over my fears about speaking in public

Which action steps do you need to take to achieve your goal?

A) *Google ways to get over fears*

B) *Check library for books on public speaking*

C) *Research Toastmasters or a speaking coach*

D) *Volunteer to give presentation*

For **Goal #1** write your powerful personal statement below. Refer to the Sample Powerful Personal Statement Ideas page if needed. After you have written your statement, ask yourself the following questions:

Personal Statement: It's easy for me to get over my fear of speaking and I feel great.

√   Is it stated in the present?
√   Is it positive?
√   Is it simple?
√   Is it believable?
√   Does it feel true?
√   Does it have a reward?

Read your personal statement out loud three times. Ask yourself honestly how you feel reading the statement. On a scale of 1 to 100 percent, how believable is it? Notice what thoughts come up for you. Remember to pay attention to your thoughts as they may point to some personal resistance.

If it's not believable, write it again below, adding the 5 Powerful Words.

"I like the idea that..."

I like the idea that it's easy for me to get over my fear of speaking and I feel great.

Read both statements and write the one that feels most true for you here: _____

_____

_____

REMINDERS

- Repeat your powerful personal statement ten times in the morning and ten times in the evening.
- Continue every day while you are working on action steps A, B, C, and D. (If you find an action step difficult, create a Powerful Personal Statement to help you complete it.)
- Write down your powerful personal statement as an exercise for reinforcement.
- Use the Widescreen TV Technique, or create your own technique. It's important to feel how good it will feel when you reach your goal. Any way you do this is fine as long as you elicit that wonderful feeling.
- Remember: SEE, FEEL, and HEAR yourself as if you have already achieved your goal.

After you have completed your goal, or your actions have become so natural that you no longer need to reinforce them, give yourself a pat on the back and move on to your next goal.

Now that you understand the steps to creating your powerful personal statement, you are ready to get started!

What do you want to do that you have put off? What would you like to accomplish this month? What would you like to achieve this year?

Grab a pen right now and write down three things that you would like to do in the space below. It doesn't matter if your goals are frivolous or serious.

If you prefer, you can print out extra worksheets here: http://www.PowerfulThinkingOnPurpose.com/worksheet

PERSONAL WORKSHEET

THREE GOALS I WANT TO ACHIEVE

1. _____

2. _____

3. _____

Write Goal #1 below. Think of ways you can break it down into small action steps and write them below too:

GOAL # 1: _____

What action steps do you need to take to achieve your goal?

A) _____

B) _____

C) _____

D) _____

For **Goal #1** write your powerful personal statement below. Refer to the Sample Powerful Personal Statement Ideas page if needed. After you have written your statement, ask yourself the following questions:

Personal Statement:

_____

_____

√   Is it stated in the present?
√   Is it positive?
√   Is it simple?
√   Is it believable?
√   Does it feel true?
√   Does it have a reward?

Read your personal statement out loud three times. Ask yourself honestly how you feel reading the above statement. On a scale of 1 to 100 percent, how believable is it? Notice what thoughts come up for you. Remember that whatever thoughts you notice may point to some personal resistance.

If it's not believable, write it again below, adding the 5 Powerful Words.

"I like the idea that…"

_____

_____

Read both statements and write the one that feels most true for you here:

REMINDERS

- Repeat your powerful personal statement ten times in the morning and ten times in the evening.
- Continue every day while you are working on action steps A, B, C, and D. (If you find an action step difficult, create a Powerful Personal Statement to help you complete it.)
- Write down your powerful personal statement as an exercise for reinforcement.
- Use the Widescreen TV Technique, or create your own technique. It's important to feel how good it will feel when you reach your goal. Any way you do this is fine as long as you elicit that wonderful feeling.
- Remember: SEE, FEEL, and HEAR yourself as if you have already achieved your goal.

REMINDER: you can print out extra worksheets here: http://www.PowerfulThinkingOnPurpose.com/worksheet

After you have completed your goal or your actions have become so natural that you no longer need to reinforce them, give yourself a pat on the back and move on to your next goal. Please remember that it's normal to have negative thoughts, it's what you do with them that makes all the difference.

Now, get out there and do great things!

ACKNOWLEDGMENTS

I'm going to tell you a secret that will make you smile. I had been putting off writing this part of my book for quite a while because I thought it would be hard to write. Then I remembered to say these words to myself: "I like the idea that writing this part of my book is easy." After I said my powerful personal statement to myself, writing these acknowledgments was easy.

Even though I'm helping others to train their thoughts every day, it's often easy to forget to be aware of my thoughts. If you find yourself forgetting, that's OK. It's human nature to be unaware of many of our thoughts. It will be easy for you to remember again, and you can continue to intentionally direct your thoughts.

A big thank you to the awesome women who have supported me and have continued to be my friends through thick and thin: Avis Yuni, Valerie Holiday, Becky Wagner, Holly Henry, and Wendy Young. Each one is a delightful person whom I feel grateful to call my friend.

A number of wonderful teachers have guided my path: Jeannie Bengston, who taught the Silva Mind Control class back in 1980 in Philadelphia; David Crump, who facilitated the Essential Experience Workshop in 2001; and my instructors and colleagues at The National Guild of Hypnotists.

Years ago I heard that we learn more by teaching than by being taught. I now understand that to be true. Thank you to all my past, present, and future students. You are so appreciated.

Thank you to those who read early drafts of my book. Not once did you make fun of my ideas or writing skills and I am very grateful. Instead, Chrissa Merron, Louisa O'Neal, Jules Merron, Dianna Harris, and Julia Ware offered sound advice that was invaluable.

A warm loving thank you to my daughters, Ariel and Maddie Goldenthal. I have learned so much from you and I am grateful to be your mom.

A huge thank you goes to Dave Braxton. He is a great friend, mentor, and business partner. I treasure our Tuesday meetings.

My editor, Ariel Goldenthal, was extremely patient and did a fantastic job at editing and formatting my book. Holly Henry greatly improved my attempt to draw readers in through the words on the back cover of this book.

Last, I want to thank Dr. Lisa Halpin, my coach, friend, and mentor who made sure my book was consistent and accurate. She is an amazing person with the insight of a dozen wise souls. She always understood exactly what I wanted to convey, and edited with gentleness, humor, and insight. Lisa is an amazing person with many talents. Everyone, including me, who comes in contact with Lisa is blessed.

Oh yes. I want to thank *you* for reading my book. I encourage you to practice and share what you have learned.

I like the idea YOU can change your life with Powerful Thinking! :-)

55680861R00086

Made in the USA
San Bernardino, CA
04 November 2017